The Mash and Smash Cookbook

Fun and Yummy Recipes Every Kid Can Make!

Marian Buck-Murray

Illustrations by Ralph Butler

John Wiley & Sons, Inc.

New York • Chichester • Weinheim • Brisbane • Singapore • Toronto

The publisher and the author have made every reasonable effort to
ensure that the experiments and activities in this book are safe when
conducted as instructed but assume no responsibility for any damage
caused or sustained while performing the experiments or activities in
the book. Parents, guardians, and/or teachers should supervise young
readers who undertake the experiments and activities in this book.

Library of Congress Cataloging-in-Publication Data
Buck-Murray, Marian.
   The mash and smash cookbook : fun and yummy recipes every
kid can make! / Marian Buck-Murray ; illustrations by Ralph Butler.
      p.   cm.
   Includes index.
   Summary: Presents fifty quick, easy, and healthy recipes that
young people can make with little or no need for dangerous equipment.
   ISBN 0-471-17969-8
   1. Cookery—Juvenile literature. [1. Cookery.] I. Butler, Ralph,
ill. II. Title.
TX652.5.B746 1998
641.5'123—dc21   97-10746

Printed in the United States of America
10 9 8 7 6 5 4 3 2 1

For my niece, Bethany Alwa—
the original after-school chef.

ACKNOWLEDGMENTS

A million special thanks to my daughter
and Master Taste Tester, Annika, and to
my budding Junior Chef, Rosalie.

Special thanks also to my many young
Mash and Smash testers: Charlotte,
Timmy, and Lizey Burkly; Karen and
Katie Haas; Rachel and Emi Ithen; the
kids and counselors at Maplewood's Camp
Prospect; and the kids at the Roseland
Free Public Library.

Sincere thanks also to my agent,
Sheree Bykofsky, and to my editors,
Kate Bradford, Kara Raezer, and Marcia
Samuels, for all their careful and
insightful guidance.

And grateful thanks to my husband,
Tom, and to my parents, Tom and Jo, for
all their patient help with this book.

Contents

Introduction

About This Book

What do a Squishwich, a Nanaberry Smash, and a Bubbling Yo-Yo have in common? They're all nutritious, kid-safe recipes that taste great. Best of all, these Mash and Smash recipes are a blast to make! You'll squish them, smash them, and shake them up to make them.

And there's more. Some of the Mash and Smash recipes will teach you kid-safe cooking skills so you can mash, bash, pound, squeeze, smush, and bubble up some very tasty treats. Other recipes are just plain quick and easy. And you won't need to use sharp knives or mixers or blenders for any of them. *The Mash and Smash Cookbook* is bursting with fun, do-it-yourself recipes for kids who love to play with their food!

Many of the Mash and Smash recipes are safe and easy enough for you to make by yourself, without adult help. These recipes are marked with **one hand** and are at the beginning of each chapter. Other Mash and Smash recipes are a little bit harder. If you're new to cooking you'll need an adult around to keep an eye on things. These recipes are marked with **two hands** and are in the middle of each chapter. To make the recipes marked with **three hands,** you will need adult help. All of the Supper Stuff recipes require adult help. In the other chapters the three-hand recipes are at the end of the chapter.

When you make these recipes, you will not need to use the toaster oven, stove, oven, or any sharp tools, or open any cans.

When you make these recipes, you might need to use the toaster oven or a sharp tool such as a vegetable peeler or cheese grater, or open a can. If you're new to cooking, ask an adult to supervise.

You'll be able to do most of the steps in these recipes by yourself, but you'll need adult help to use the oven and stove.

Throughout this book, you'll find helpful hints for how to do the recipes and interesting facts about the ingredients you're using. Some recipes also have suggestions about how to invent your own awesome food creations.

Before you begin any of the recipes, be sure to read through this introduction completely, especially the "How to Make a Mash and Smash Recipe" section below. You'll also find important information about safety rules, ingredients, tools, and skills in this introduction.

Then, when you're ready to begin, roll up your sleeves, and smash, mash, bash, squish, smush, and shake up some fun!

How to Make a Mash and Smash Recipe

1. Ask an adult for permission to use the kitchen.
2. Clear a work space on the kitchen table or counter and wipe it off with a wet sponge or cloth. (Keep this sponge handy to wipe up any spills.)
3. Wash your hands.
4. Read through "Mash and Smash Safety Rules," page 4.
5. Read completely through the recipe you want to make. Remember that recipes marked with two and three hands require adult supervision.
6. Gather all the ingredients you will need to make the recipe. If you don't have all of the ingredients, choose another recipe.
7. Gather all the tools you will need to make the recipe. Check "Mash and Smash Tools" on page 6 if you're not sure what certain tools are.

8. Make your recipe one step at a time, adding the ingredients in the order they are listed. Ingredients appear in **boldface** type the first time they are used in a recipe. Always check the list of ingredients above the instructions for the correct amounts. Check "Mash and Smash Skills" on page 9 if you're not sure how to do certain steps. Never perform steps yourself that call for an adult helper.

9. When you're finished, clean up the kitchen so you'll be allowed to use it again!

How to Invent a Recipe

Throughout this book you'll find suggestions for ways to create your very own recipes. Be sure to follow these steps each time you invent a recipe.

1. Look in cookbooks to get ideas for your recipe.

2. Write a list of ingredients that you think will taste good in your recipe.

3. Write down different combinations of recipe ingredients until you come up with a combination you think will work.

4. Make your recipe and write down the amount of each ingredient as you use it. Look at similar recipes to get ideas about the amounts to use.

5. Write down every tool you use to make your recipe.

6. Write down everything you do to your ingredients to make them into a recipe.

7. Taste your recipe. Keep the recipe if you like it, and make it again another time.

8. If you don't like your recipe, decide what you don't like. Next, think up ways to make it better. Then try again!

Mash and Smash Safety Rules

1. Ask an adult to help you choose the best recipe level for you.
2. If you're new to cooking, ask an adult to supervise when you do any recipe marked with two hands. Have an adult help you do the recipes marked with three hands.
3. Always wash your hands before and after cooking, especially when using eggs, raw meat, or raw chicken.
4. Never taste anything that contains raw egg, raw meat, or raw chicken.
5. Wash fresh fruits and vegetables before using them in a recipe.
6. Always use clean tools.
7. Always wear thick oven mitts when you use the toaster oven, stove, or oven. Be sure to turn off the toaster oven, stove, or oven when you're finished cooking.
8. Don't let the handles of pots and pans hang out over the edge of the stove.
9. Place hot pans on top of the stove, not on the counter.
10. Let hot food cool before eating it.
11. When using a knife or a vegetable peeler, always cut away from yourself and toward the cutting board. Pick up knives by the handle and always use a cutting board. Never try to catch a falling knife.

Mash and Smash Ingredients

Mash and Smash recipes use plenty of fresh fruits and vegetables, bread, cheese, milk, and yogurt. Here's a list of other things you'll need to have on hand to make the recipes in this book.

Pantry and Refrigerator/Freezer Items

canned beans

canned corn

canned tomatoes and
    tomato paste

dried milk

frozen berries (blueberries,
    strawberries, raspberries)

frozen juice concentrates (apple,
    orange, grape)

frozen vegetables (corn, chopped
    peppers, mixed vegetables, green
    vegetables)

honey

jam (blueberry, strawberry, raspberry)

maple syrup

peanut butter (unsweetened)

salsa

seltzer

soft flour tortillas

spaghetti sauce

tuna fish

wheat germ

Leftovers

baked potatoes

cooked pasta

cooked rice

mashed potatoes

Mash and Smash Tools

Tools for Mixing, Mashing, Smashing, Bashing, Shaking, and Other Fun Skills

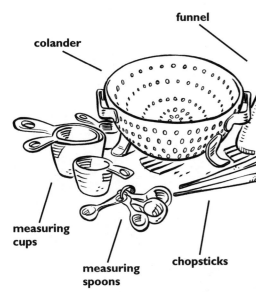

colander
funnel
measuring cups
measuring spoons
chopsticks

beverage pitcher A 2- to 3-quart container with a spout used to pour liquids into smaller containers.

can opener A tool used to open metal cans.

chopsticks A pair of thin sticks used to eat food, particularly in Asian countries. Use bamboo skewers if you don't have chopsticks.

colander A large bowl with lots of small holes, used for rinsing and draining foods.

fork A fork used as an eating utensil at the table.

funnel A small hollow cone with a tube at on end, used to pour things from large containers into small containers.

measuring cups Cups with clear measurement markings on the sides. Some have spouts for easy pouring.

measuring spoons Spoons of different sizes used to measure small amounts of food. They usually come in a set of 1 tablespoon, $\frac{1}{2}$ tablespoon, 1 teaspoon, $\frac{1}{2}$ teaspoon, and $\frac{1}{4}$ teaspoon.

mixing bowls Small, medium, and large round-bottomed bowls.

mixing bowls
plastic containers
plastic bags
Popsicle molds

plastic bags Clean 1-quart and 1-gallon resealable plastic bags and 1-gallon plastic storage bags. Wash your plastic bags so that you can use them again and again.

plastic containers with lids Containers of various sizes used to shake up ingredients and store leftovers.

Popsicle molds Small individual plastic molds used for freezing yogurt and ice cream. Use paper cups if you don't have molds.

rolling pin A wooden or plastic roller used to flatten foods.

spoons
  large serving spoon A spoon used for serving food at the table.
  small spoon A spoon used as an eating utensil at the table.
  wooden spoon A large spoon used to stir hot and cold ingredients.

squeeze bottles Plastic bottles with nozzle-shaped tops, which can be purchased at crafts stores and restaurant supply stores. Cut off part of the tip of the bottle to squeeze out thick liquids.

wire whisk A wire tool used to beat foods by hand.

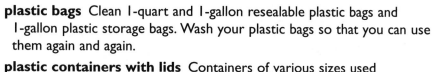

squeeze bottle

wire whisk

wooden spoon

small spoon

rolling pin

large serving spoon

Tools for Snipping, Cutting, Grating, and Peeling

cutting board A wooden or plastic board that provides a surface on which to cut or peel foods.

grater A tool with sharp-edged surface holes, used to grate and shred foods like cheese or carrots into tiny pieces.

safety scissors Metal or plastic craft scissors with blunt ends.

table knife A knife with a dull blade used as a utensil at the table.

vegetable peeler A hand-held tool used to remove the skin from fruits and vegetables.

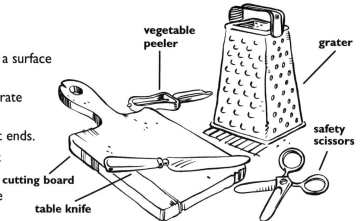

vegetable peeler

grater

safety scissors

cutting board

table knife

Tools for Cooking and Baking

basting brush A kitchen tool that looks like a paintbrush, used to brush liquids onto foods or pans.

oven mitts Thick padded mittens worn for protection when handling hot pots and pans.

paper baking cups Oven-safe paper cups used for baking muffins and cupcakes.

pots and pans

baking dish A round or rectangular glass or ceramic pan used for baking foods in the oven.

baking pan A rectangular or square glass or metal pan with high sides, used for baking foods in the oven.

broiler pan A large rectangular or oval pan with a rack, used for broiling meat.

cookie sheet A flat rectangular pan with no sides or low sides, used for baking cookies and other foods.

griddle A flat round or square pan with no sides, used for cooking pancakes.

muffin tin A metal pan with small round cups, used for baking muffins and cupcakes.

pie pan A round metal or glass pan with low sides, used for baking pies.

2-quart and 3-quart heavy-bottomed pots with lids Used for cooking food on the stove.

skillet A round pan with low sides and a handle, used for cooking and frying foods.

pot

skillet

baking pans

basting brush

baking dish

cookie sheet

toaster oven

oven mitt

spatula

$1\frac{1}{2}$- to $2\frac{1}{2}$-gallon soup pot Used for cooking soups and stews.

spatula A flat tool used for lifting and turning foods.

timer A kitchen tool used to time the number of minutes needed to bake or cook a food.

Mash and Smash Skills

cracking eggs Crack an egg by gently tapping it against the rim of a small empty bowl. Next, use your fingers to carefully open the eggshell and pour the egg into the bowl. If the egg smells bad, throw it away. Remove any eggshell pieces. Use a fork to mix together the egg yolk and white before adding the egg to other recipe ingredients.

cutting Always cut food on a cutting board. Using a table knife, cut away from yourself and toward the cutting board.

draining beans Use a can opener to open the can of beans. Put a colander in the sink and pour the beans into the colander to drain off the liquid. Rinse the beans with cold water. Measure the correct amount of beans. Pour the leftover beans into a plastic container and store them in the refrigerator.

grating and shredding Use a grater to grate or shred cheese or vegetables into small pieces. The small holes are for grating food into tiny pieces. The large holes are for shredding food into tiny strips. If you are using a flat grater, place it over a bowl. If you are using an upright grater, put it on a cutting board. Keeping your fingers away from the surface of the grater, hold one end of the food and press the other end against the holes of the grater. Pressing hard, rub the food back and

forth, or up and down, against the grater. The grated food will fall into the bowl or onto the cutting board. Stop grating when the piece of food becomes too small to grate. Repeat with more pieces until you have grated the correct amount.

greasing pans Grease pans and cookie sheets before baking so the baked food will be easy to remove. Put about 1 teaspoon of margarine on a small piece of waxed paper. Rub the waxed paper over the surface of the pan until it is covered completely with a thin layer of margarine.

measuring dry ingredients Pour or spoon the ingredient into the measuring cup or spoon, filling it up to the edge. Use a table knife to level off the ingredient. When measuring brown sugar, be sure to pack, or press, it down.

measuring wet ingredients Set a clear glass or plastic measuring cup on the table or counter. Carefully pour or spoon the ingredient into the measuring cup, filling it to the correct measuring line. Check what you've measured by looking at it at eye level to make sure it's accurate.

peeling Use a vegetable peeler to peel the skin off fruits and vegetables. Put your hand on one end of the food, holding it at an angle on a cutting board. Use the vegetable peeler to peel the food away from yourself and toward the cutting board. Peel off all or most of the outer skin.

thawing frozen juice concentrate Measure out the correct amount of concentrate and put it into a bowl or cup. Let it sit at room temperature for 5 to 10 minutes, or until it thaws.

To thaw concentrate in the microwave oven, put the correct amount in a microwave-safe bowl. Put the bowl in the microwave and heat on low or defrost for 20 to 30 seconds. Store any unused juice concentrate in a plastic container in the freezer.

Mash and Smash Measurements

3 teaspoons = 1 tablespoon

4 tablespoons = $\frac{1}{4}$ cup

8 tablespoons = $\frac{1}{2}$ cup

12 tablespoons = $\frac{3}{4}$ cup

16 tablespoons = 1 cup

1 cup = 8 ounces

2 cups = 16 ounces = 1 pint

4 cups = 32 ounces = 1 quart

4 quarts = 128 ounces = 1 gallon

1 cup shredded cheese = 4 ounces cheese

juice of one lemon = 3 tablespoons lemon juice

1 cup dry rice = 3 cups cooked rice

$\frac{1}{2}$ pound dry spaghetti = 4 cups cooked spaghetti

Breakfast Bites

The recipes in this chapter will add some scrumptious fun to your mornings. At the beginning of the chapter you'll find quick and easy recipes for school-day breakfasts. At the end of the chapter you'll find the more challenging recipes to make with your family on sleepy weekend mornings. Don't forget to try the Invent-a-Recipe on page 15!

WHAT'S INSIDE:

- ▶ Wake Up Shake-Up
- ▶ Monday's Sundae
- ▶ Graham Cracker Soup
- ▶ Honey Cream Squeeze
- ▶ Nutty Honey Rollers
- ▶ French Fingers
- ▶ Scrambled French Toast
- ▶ Rosalie's Corn Muffins
- ▶ Grandma Jo's Granola
- ▶ Scribble Cake Mix
- ▶ Scribble Cakes

Wake Up Shake-Up

Shake up your morning with this yogurt and banana milk shake.

Makes 1 to 2 servings

Ingredients	Tools	
1 small ripe banana	small mixing bowl	measuring cups
$\frac{1}{2}$ cup plain or vanilla yogurt	1-gallon plastic bag	measuring spoons
$\frac{1}{2}$ cup milk	small spoon	large drinking glass
1 tablespoon jam	1-quart plastic container with lid	straw
1 teaspoon sugar		

TIP

For an even quicker Wake Up Shake-Up, make the recipe with 2 tablespoons of jam and no banana.

1. Peel the **banana** and break it into three or four pieces. Put the banana pieces in the bowl.

2. Put your hand in the plastic bag. Use your bagged hand to squish and smush the banana. Keep squishing and smushing until the banana is well smushed.

3. Spoon the smushed banana into the plastic container.

4. Add the **yogurt, milk, jam,** and **sugar.** Put the lid on the plastic container, and seal it tightly.

5. Put your hand on the lid of the plastic container and shake it up and down as hard as you can. Jump up and down! Shake until the mixture is well mixed.

6. Pour your Wake Up Shake-Up into the large glass. Serve with a straw and wake up!

Invent-a-Recipe

Invent your own Shake-Up! It can be fruity and juicy, rich and creamy, or very, very thick. In place of the ingredients in this recipe, you can use any combination you like of fruits, juices, yogurt, milk, ice cream, syrups, jellies, jams, herbal teas, and special flavors. Then shake them up and drink up!

Monday's Sundae

Here's a sweet and crunchy yogurt sundae for Monday—or any other day.

Makes 1 serving

Ingredients

$\frac{1}{2}$ cup plain or vanilla yogurt

1 tablespoon honey, maple syrup, or jam

suggested toppings: 1 to 2 table-spoons of wheat germ, crunchy cereal, granola, coconut, raisins, blueberries, strawberries

Tools

measuring cup

small bowl

measuring spoons

---

1. Put the **yogurt** into the bowl.

2. Top the yogurt with **honey, maple syrup,** or **jam.**

3. Sprinkle on one or more of the suggested toppings, and serve.

Graham Cracker Soup

Makes I serving

Get ready to pound and smash the ingredients for this yummy breakfast soup!

Ingredients		Tools
I plain rice cake	I shake cinnamon	I-quart sturdy resealable plastic bag
I graham cracker (2 squares)	milk (about $\frac{1}{4}$ cup)	cereal bowl

TiP

To reuse a plastic bag, use a soapy sponge to wash the inside and outside. Then rinse the bag thoroughly with water and use a towel to dry.

More than 2 million dairy cows live and work in the state of Wisconsin. They eat lots of grass and make lots of milk. In fact, they make so much milk that they need more than 44,000 farmers to milk them twice a day, every day.

1. Put the **rice cake, graham cracker,** and **cinnamon** into the plastic bag. Push the air out of the bag and seal it tightly.

2. Use your fists to gently pound and smash the rice cake and graham cracker in the bag.

3. Shake the bag up and down.

4. Pour the smashed mixture into the cereal bowl.

5. Add **milk** and serve.

Honey Cream Squeeze

Here's a sweet and creamy spread to squish and squeeze.

Makes 4 to 6 servings

Ingredients	Tools
4 ounces cream cheese	measuring spoons
2 tablespoons honey	1-gallon plastic bag with twist tie
bread or toast	safety scissors
	table knife
	small plastic container with lid

TiP

Rub a little bit of oil on your tablespoon before measuring the honey. This will help the honey slide easily off the spoon.

1. Put the **cream cheese** and the **honey** into the plastic bag. Push all of the air out of the bag. Close the top of the bag with the twist tie.

2. Squish and smush the cream cheese and honey in the bag until they are completely smushed together. Be careful not to break the bag.

3. Squeeze all of the honey cream mixture to the bottom of the bag.

4. Wash and dry the safety scissors.

5. Use the scissors to cut a very small hole from the bottom corner of the plastic bag.

6. Squeeze the bag to put a little of the honey cream on a slice of **bread.** Spread with the table knife.

7. Put the bag of Honey Cream Squeeze in the plastic container and store it in the refrigerator until you're ready to squeeze again.

HONEY

Nutty Honey Rollers

These nutty tortilla roll-ups are sticky-lickin' good.

Makes 1 to 2 servings

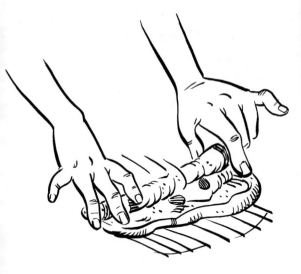

Ingredients	Tools	
1 soft tortilla	toaster oven	oven mitts
peanut butter (about 1 tablespoon)	foil	timer
honey (1 to 2 teaspoons)	safety scissors	spatula
2 teaspoons raisins	table knife	plate
	measuring spoons	

1. Remove the tray from the toaster oven. Cover it with foil and set it aside.

2. Preheat the toaster oven to medium broil.

3. Wash and dry the safety scissors.

4. Use the scissors to cut the **tortilla** in half.

5. Use the table knife to lightly spread **peanut butter** on each tortilla half.

6. Lightly spread **honey** over the peanut butter on each tortilla half.

7. Sprinkle 1 teaspoon of **raisins** on each half.

8. Roll up the tortillas so they look like small, thick sticks. Place them on the foil-covered toaster oven tray.

9. Put on the oven mitts to put the tray back in the toaster oven.

10. Broil the Nutty Honey Rollers for 3 to 5 minutes. Watch carefully!

11. Wearing oven mitts, use the spatula to remove the Nutty Honey Rollers from the toaster oven and put them on the plate. (Be sure to turn off the toaster oven.)

12. Let your Nutty Honey Rollers cool for 1 to 2 minutes before serving.

TiP

Try using cinnamon and honey, or jelly and cream cheese, in place of the ingredients in this recipe. Yum!

French Fingers

Use your fingers to eat these sweet French toast fingers.

Makes 1 to 2 servings

The Algonquin, Iroquois, and Ojibway tribes living in northeastern North America were the first to make pure maple syrup. During the spring they tapped maple trees by cutting them with light axes called tomahawks. They used wooden dishes to collect the sap, the liquid that pours out of the trees. The Native Americans cooked the maple sap in hollowed-out logs until it turned into dark, thick maple syrup.

Ingredients
- 2 slices bread
- 1 egg
- 1 tablespoon milk
- 1 tablespoon maple syrup
- 2 shakes cinnamon

Tools
- toaster oven
- foil
- cutting board
- table knife
- small mixing bowl
- fork
- measuring spoons
- oven mitts
- timer
- spatula

1. Remove the tray from the toaster oven. Cover the tray with foil and set it aside.

2. Preheat the toaster oven to medium broil.

3. On the cutting board, use the table knife to cut each slice of **bread** into 3 strips, or "fingers." Set aside.

4. Crack the **egg** into the bowl. Mix the egg well with the fork.

5. Add the **milk, maple syrup,** and **cinnamon** to the bowl. Mix well with the fork.

6. Dip each bread finger into the egg mixture, turning the bread fingers over to coat both sides completely. Put the bread fingers on the foil-covered toaster oven tray. (Remember to wash your hands when you're finished.)

7. Put on the oven mitts, and put the toaster oven tray back into the toaster oven.

8. Broil the French Fingers for 3 minutes.

9. Wearing the oven mitts, use the spatula to carefully turn over each bread finger.

10. Broil for another 3 minutes. Wearing the oven mitts, remove the tray from the toaster oven. Put it on top of the toaster oven or on the stove. (Be sure to turn off the toaster oven.) Let cool for 1 minute before serving.

TiP

To cook French Fingers on the stove, you'll need to ask an adult to help you. First, follow steps 3 though 6. Next, use a basting brush to lightly oil a griddle or skillet. Heat the griddle on the stove for 1 to 2 minutes over medium high heat. Add the French Fingers to the skillet. Cook for 3 to 4 minutes, or until golden brown. Use a spatula to turn the French Fingers, and cook for 3 to 4 minutes more. Let cool for 1 minute before serving.

Scrambled French Toast

Makes 2 servings

Here's a mixed-up way to make a tasty favorite.

Ingredients	Tools	
2 eggs	small mixing bowl	small skillet
2 slices bread	fork	wooden spoon
$\frac{1}{4}$ cup milk	measuring cups	timer
2 tablespoons maple syrup or brown sugar	measuring spoons	adult helper
2 shakes cinnamon	basting brush	
2 teaspoons vegetable oil		

The average hen lays 200 eggs a year!

1. Carefully crack the **eggs** into the bowl. Use the fork to mix well.

2. Tear the **bread** into small pieces. Put them in the bowl. Mix well with the fork.

3. Add the **milk, maple syrup,** and **cinnamon** to the bowl, and mix well. Put the bowl next to the stove.

4. Pour the **oil** into a clean measuring cup. Dip the basting brush into the oil, then brush a thin layer of oil onto the bottom of the skillet.

5. Ask your adult helper to heat the skillet on the stove over medium heat for about 30 seconds.

6. Add the egg-bread mixture to the skillet. Scramble with the wooden spoon until the mixture is lightly browned and no longer wet, about 5 minutes.

7. Have the adult remove the skillet from the stove. Let your Scrambled French Toast cool for 1 to 2 minutes before serving.

Rosalie's Corn Muffins

Makes 12 muffins

Your family will be crazy about these corny muffins.

Ingredients	Tools	
1 teaspoon margarine	measuring cups	small mixing bowl
1 cup cornmeal	measuring spoons	fork
1 cup flour	small piece of waxed paper	paper towel
$\frac{1}{2}$ cup sugar		oven mitts
1 tablespoon baking powder	muffin tin	timer
$\frac{1}{2}$ teaspoon salt	large mixing bowl	table knife
1 cup milk	large spoon	adult helper
2 tablespoons vegetable oil		
1 egg		

1. Preheat the oven to 375°F.

2. Grease the muffin tin by using a small piece of the waxed paper to rub a little bit of **margarine** in each muffin tin cup.

3. Put the **cornmeal, flour, sugar, baking powder,** and **salt** in the large mixing bowl. Use the large spoon to stir well.

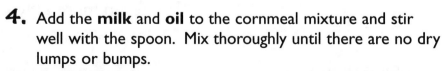

4. Add the **milk** and **oil** to the cornmeal mixture and stir well with the spoon. Mix thoroughly until there are no dry lumps or bumps.

5. Crack the **egg** into the small bowl. Mix well with the fork.

6. Add the egg to the cornmeal mixture. Stir well with the large spoon.

7. Use the large spoon to put 2 spoonfuls of cornmeal batter into each muffin tin cup. Use a paper towel to wipe up any drips left on the muffin tin.

8. Have an adult put the muffin tin in the oven. Bake the muffins for 15 minutes.

9. Have an adult remove the muffin tin from the oven when the muffins are done. Let them cool for 10 minutes before removing them from the muffin tin.

TiP

To test a muffin for doneness, stick a table knife into its center. If the knife comes out clean, the muffins are done. If the knife comes out gooky, you'll need to bake the muffins for about 5 minutes more.

Grandma Jo's Granola

Here's an incredibly delicious granola recipe for you to get your hands into.

Makes about 5 cups granola

Ingredients		Tools
$\frac{1}{2}$ cup wheat bran	$\frac{1}{2}$ cup dried milk	measuring cups
$\frac{1}{2}$ cup wheat germ	3 cups rolled oats	large mixing bowl
$\frac{1}{2}$ cup whole wheat flour	$\frac{1}{2}$ cup vegetable oil, plus extra oil for hands	wooden spoon
$\frac{1}{2}$ cup sesame seeds	$\frac{3}{4}$ cup honey	large baking pan
		oven mitts
		timer
		1 or 2 large plastic containers
		adult helper

1. Preheat the oven to 300°F.

2. Put the **bran, wheat germ, whole wheat flour, sesame seeds, dried milk,** and **oats** into the large mixing bowl. Use your hands to mix all of the ingredients together.

3. Add $\frac{1}{2}$ cup of the **oil** and all of the **honey.**

4. Rub a little bit of extra oil onto your hands. Use your oiled hands to mix together all of the ingredients in the bowl. (You might want to ask a friend to help.) Mix until all of the ingredients are well combined. Really dig in!

Harvey Kellogg, the inventor of Kellogg's Corn Flakes, also invented the very first granola, in 1881.

5. Ask an adult to tip the bowl as you use the wooden spoon to pour the granola into the baking pan. Spread the granola evenly over the bottom of the pan.

6. Have the adult put the pan into the oven. Set the timer for 10 minutes.

7. After 10 minutes, have the adult carefully pull out the baking pan. Wearing oven mitts, use a wooden spoon to stir the granola. Stir it so that the granola on the bottom ends up on top. This helps prevent burning.

8. Bake the granola for another 20 to 30 minutes, repeating step 7 every 10 minutes.

9 When finished, have the adult remove the granola from the oven.

10. Let the granola cool for 10 to 15 minutes, then sprinkle on cereal, yogurt, or ice cream.

11. Store extra granola in the plastic containers.

Scribble Cake Mix

Makes about 6 cups (3 batches)

What's white flour? It's wheat that's missing the bran and germ found in whole wheat. The bran is the shell of the wheat grain that protects the inside of the grain. It's rich in the fiber that helps scrub your insides clean. The germ is the part of the grain that grows into a new plant. It gives you energy and vitamins to make you strong. With both the bran and germ, the whole wheat found in whole wheat flour is much better for you than the naked wheat in white flour.

Mix up your very own easy-to-use pancake mix.

Ingredients		Tools
2 cups white flour	1 tablespoon baking powder	measuring cups
2 cups whole wheat flour	2 teaspoons salt	measuring spoons
1 cup wheat germ		1-gallon resealable plastic bag
1 cup cornmeal		
$\frac{1}{2}$ cup sugar		

1. Put the **white flour, whole wheat flour, wheat germ, cornmeal, sugar, baking powder,** and **salt** into the plastic bag. Push the air from the bag and seal it.

2. Turn the bag over and over, to dump the pancake mix from one end to the other, until it is completely mixed together. Really mix it up!

3. Label the bag and store your pancake mix in the freezer until you're ready to use it. (See Scribble Cakes, page 31, to learn how to make your pancakes.)

Scribble Cakes

Makes 4 servings

Use this batter to squeeze and scribble some pancakes in any wacky shape you can think of.

Ingredients	Tools	
2 cups Scribble Cake Mix (page 30)	measuring cups	plastic squeeze bottle
$1\frac{1}{2}$ cups milk	measuring spoons	basting brush
2 tablespoons vegetable oil, plus extra oil for griddle	large beverage pitcher	large griddle
	wooden spoon	spatula
	small mixing bowl	oven-safe dinner plate
2 eggs	fork	oven mitts
		adult helper

1. Preheat the oven to warm.

2. Put the **Scribble Cake Mix, milk,** and 2 tablespoons of **oil** into the pitcher. Stir well with the wooden spoon, making sure to get all the gooky lumps and bumps off the sides and the bottom of the pitcher.

3. Crack the **eggs** into the bowl. Mix well with the fork.

4. Pour the mixed egg into the pitcher and stir well with the wooden spoon.

5. Pour the pancake batter into the plastic squeeze bottle to fill the bottle. Close the squeeze bottle tightly. (You will

Use scissors to snip off part of the tip of the squeeze bottle. This will help the batter squeeze easily through the hole.

TiP

have pancake batter left in the pitcher.)

6. Pour a little bit of oil (about 1 tablespoon) into a clean measuring cup. Dip the basting brush into the oil. Brush the griddle lightly with oil.

7. Ask an adult to heat the griddle on the stove over medium low heat for 1 to 2 minutes.

8. Squeeze the batter onto the griddle and scribble a wacky animal or a crazy design. Make two or three pancakes, leaving 1 to 2 inches between pancakes so they don't run into each other.

9. When the tops of the pancakes are completely covered with bubbles (about 3 to 4 minutes), have the adult help you use the spatula to turn them.

10. Cook the pancakes 1 or 2 minutes longer, or until they are golden brown on both sides. When they're done, use the spatula to move them from the griddle to the plate. Wearing the oven mitts, put the plate in the oven to keep the pancakes warm.

11. Repeat steps 7 to 10 with the rest of the pancake batter. Brush the griddle with oil after each set of pancakes. Refill the squeeze bottle as needed.

2

Goodwiches

Goodwiches are great do-it-yourself sandwiches. They're perfect for school lunch boxes and lazy Saturday afternoons. Some are crunchy, and some are squishy. Some are big, and some are bitsy. A few of them don't even look like sandwiches at all! The recipes in this chapter are all marked with one or two hands, so pick one with your favorite lunch flavors, and dig in. Be sure to try the Invent-a-Recipe on page 47.

What's Inside:

▶ B'namich
▶ Squishwich
▶ Apple Cruncher
▶ Dreamwich
▶ Sandwich Kabobs
▶ Annika's Tuna Wheels
▶ Tuna Cheesers
▶ Pizza Stuffers
▶ Neato B'Nito

B'namich

Here's a peanut butter and banana sandwich—without the bread.

Makes 1 serving

Ingredients	Tools
1 banana	table knife
peanut butter	cutting board
raisins	

1. Peel the **banana.** Use the table knife to cut it in half the long way on the cutting board.
2. Spread one banana half with **peanut butter** and sprinkle it with **raisins.**
3. Put the banana back together and cut it in half the short way.
4. Eat your B'namich like a sandwich.

Bananas grow on banana trees, right? Wrong. The banana plant is actually a very large herb. The stalk of the banana plant is soft, not hard like the wood and bark of a tree trunk. When the stalk is fully formed, it sprouts a huge flowering stem. Gigantic purple buds grow on this stem, and inside the buds are tiny blossoms. These tiny blossoms grow into big bananas.

Squishwich

White beans and spaghetti sauce make a deliciously squishy sandwich.

Makes 1 or 2 servings

Ingredients

$\frac{1}{3}$ cup canned white beans, drained

2 tablespoons spaghetti sauce

2 slices bread

1 piece lettuce

Tools

measuring cup

measuring spoons

small, sturdy resealable plastic bag

small spoon

table knife

1. Put the **beans** and the **spaghetti sauce** in the plastic bag. Push the air out of the bag and seal.

2. Pound and squish the sealed bag with your hands and fingers until the beans and sauce are well squished together.

3. Use the spoon to put the squished beans on one slice of **bread.** Spread the squished beans evenly over the bread with the table knife.

4. Put the **lettuce** and the other slice of bread on top of the beans. Cut your Squishwich in half, and serve.

Apple Cruncher

Nuts and apples make this cheese sandwich a crunchy munch.

Makes 1 or 2 servings

Ingredients		Tools
1 pita bread	1 small apple	cutting board
mayonnaise (about 2 teaspoons)		table knife
		measuring spoons
1 tablespoon nuts (peanuts, chopped walnuts, or slivered almonds)		small, sturdy resealable plastic bag
		rolling pin
		small spoon

1. Put the **pita bread** on the cutting board. Use the table knife to cut the pita in half.

2. Use the table knife to carefully spread a little **mayonnaise** inside each pita half.

3. Put the **nuts** into the plastic bag. Push the air out of the bag and seal it.

4. Use the rolling pin to pound and smash the nuts until they are well smashed.

5. Spoon an equal amount of smashed nuts into each pita half.

6. Put the **apple** on the cutting board. Hold the apple down with one hand while you stick the tip of the table knife into the top of the apple. Pull the knife out and cut the apple from top to bottom where you made the cut.

7. Repeat step 6 until you've cut the whole apple into big pieces.

8. Remove any seeds from the apple pieces.

9. Use the table knife to cut the apple pieces into pieces the size of marbles.

10. Spoon an equal amount of apple pieces into each pita half and serve.

Dreamwich

This creamy sandwich is a raisin-lover's dream come true.

Makes 1 or 2 servings

H ow fast can you eat a raisin? 1 second? 2 seconds? It may take only seconds to eat raisins, but it takes a lot longer to make them. Raisin farmers start by growing grapes. The grapes grow and plump for months in the hot sun until they ripen in late summer. Then they're picked and placed on paper sheets between the rows of vines, where they dry in the sun for 2 to 3 weeks until they turn into raisins. Next, the farmers roll the raisins into bundles and let them dry for several more days. Then the raisins are cleaned, packaged, and sent off to grocery stores.

Ingredients	Tools	
1 tablespoon raisins	safety scissors	small spoon
1 tablespoon cream cheese	measuring spoons	table knife
2 slices bread	small mixing bowl	

1. Wash and dry the safety scissors.

2. Use the safety scissors to snip the **raisins** into teeny pieces. Snip the raisins over the mixing bowl so that the raisin pieces fall into it.

3. Add the **cream cheese** to the raisin pieces. Stir well with the spoon.

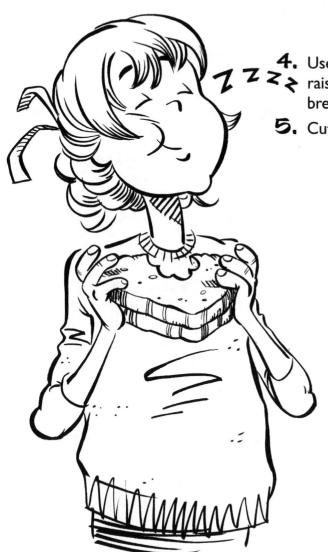

4. Use the table knife to spread one piece of **bread** with the raisin and cream cheese mixture. Put the other piece of bread on top.

5. Cut your Dreamwich in half and serve.

Sandwich Kabobs

Makes 1 or 2 servings

Here's a crazy new way to make a regular old sandwich.

Ingredients

2 slices bread

mayonnaise or mustard (about 1 tablespoon)

2 slices cheese, such as provolone or American

2 slices deli meat, such as turkey, ham, or roast beef

2 pieces lettuce

Tools

cutting board

table knife

measuring spoons

2 chopsticks

1. Put the **bread** on the cutting board. Use the table knife to cut each slice of bread into 4 squares. (First cut each slice in half, then cut each half in half.)

2. Spread **mayonnaise** or **mustard** on each bread square.

3. Carefully cut or tear each piece of **cheese, meat,** and **lettuce** into 3 pieces.

4. Hold one bread square with the mayonnaise side up, and slide it over the pointy end of the chopstick to the other end.

TIP

Make other Sandwich Kabobs by spreading bread squares with peanut butter, almond butter, cream cheese, jelly, or bean spread.

5. Slide a piece of cheese onto the chopstick, and move it down to the bread. Repeat with a piece of meat, lettuce, and another bread square.

6. Repeat step 5 two more times. On your chopstick you should have the following layers: bread, cheese, meat, lettuce; bread, cheese, meat, lettuce; bread, cheese, meat, lettuce, bread.

7. Repeat steps 4 through 6 with the second chopstick.

8. Carefully slide all the layers into the center of each chopstick.

9. Eat your Sandwich Kabob like an ear of corn-on-the-cob.

Annika's Tuna Wheels

Makes 2 servings

Roll a supercool tuna wheel right into your mouth!

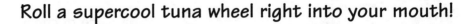

Ingredients	Tools	
1 6½-ounce can tuna fish, packed in water	can opener	measuring spoons
	colander	cutting board
2 tablespoons mayonnaise	small spoon	table knife
1 shake salt	small mixing bowl	plastic wrap
1 shake pepper	fork	
1 cucumber		

1. Use the can opener to open the can of **tuna.** Put the colander in the sink and dump the tuna into the colander to drain off the water.

2. Spoon the tuna into the bowl. Use the fork to mash well.

3. Add the **mayonnaise, salt,** and **pepper** to the tuna and stir well with the spoon.

4. Put the **cucumber** on the cutting board. Use the table knife to cut the cucumber into 5 or 6 thick slices, or wheels.

Protein is found in tuna and other fish, and in beans, eggs, meat, nuts, and cheese. Your body turns this protein into different kinds of protein it can use. Some protein is very straight and long, and makes your body parts strong. Another kind of protein is shaped like a hollow ball, and carries nutrients to your body parts. Other protein is coiled like a telephone wire. This kind helps your body parts stretch and bend. Proteins are all different to help you do all the different things you do!

5. Use the point of the spoon to scoop out the seeds from the cucumber wheels. (Don't scoop out all of the cucumber!)

6. Stuff a spoonful of the tuna mixture into each cucumber wheel and serve. (If you have any leftover tuna, cover the bowl with plastic wrap and refrigerate.)

Tuna Cheesers

Makes 1 or 2 servings

These easy tuna sandwiches are deliciously warm and cheesy.

Ingredients	Tools	
1 6½-ounce can tuna fish, packed in water	toaster oven	cutting board
2 tablespoons mayonnaise	foil	table knife
	can opener	plastic wrap
1 shake salt	colander	oven mitts
1 shake pepper	small spoon	timer
1 pita bread	small mixing bowl	spatula
2 slices of your favorite cheese	fork	plate
	measuring spoons	

1. Remove the tray from the toaster oven. Cover the tray with foil and set it aside.

2. Preheat the toaster oven to medium broil.

3. Use the can opener to open the can of tuna. Put the colander in the sink and dump the **tuna** in the colander to drain off the water.

4. Spoon the tuna into the bowl. Mash well with the fork.

5. Add the **mayonnaise, salt,** and **pepper** to the tuna and stir well with the fork.

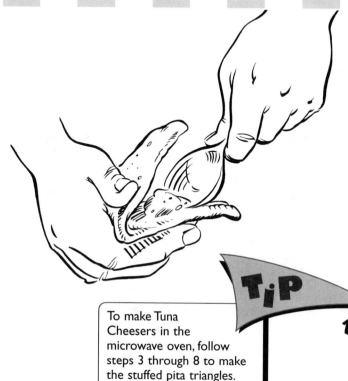

6. Put the **pita bread** on the cutting board. Use the table knife to cut the pita in half, then cut each half in half to make 4 triangles.

7. Stuff 1 tablespoon of the tuna mixture into each pita triangle. (Cover the bowl with plastic wrap and refrigerate the leftover tuna.)

8. Tear each **cheese slice** into 2 pieces. Stuff one piece of cheese into each pita triangle.

9. Put the stuffed pita triangles on the foil-covered toaster oven tray. Put on the oven mitts and put the tray back into the toaster oven.

10. Broil the Tuna Cheesers for 3 minutes, or until the cheese has melted. Watch carefully.

11. Wearing oven mitts, use the spatula to remove your Tuna Cheesers from the toaster oven and put them on the plate. (Be sure to turn off the toaster oven.) Let cool for 1 to 2 minutes, then serve.

TiP

To make Tuna Cheesers in the microwave oven, follow steps 3 through 8 to make the stuffed pita triangles. Put the triangles on a microwave-safe plate, and put the plate into the microwave. Heat on High for 1 minute, or until the cheese has melted. Wear oven mitts to remove the Tuna Cheesers from the microwave. Let cool for 1 to 2 minutes before serving.

Pizza Stuffers

Try these super pita pockets stuffed with pizza stuff.

Makes 1 or 2 servings

Ingredients	Tools	
1 pita bread	toaster oven	oven mitts
8 teaspoons spaghetti sauce or pizza sauce	foil	timer
	cutting board	spatula
	table knife	plate
2 slices cheese, such as provolone or mozzarella	measuring spoons	

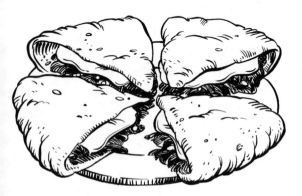

1. Remove the tray from the toaster oven. Cover it with foil and set aside.

2. Preheat the toaster oven to medium broil.

3. Put the **pita bread** on the cutting board. Use the table knife to cut the pita in half, then cut each half in half to make 4 triangles.

4. Put 2 teaspoons of **spaghetti sauce** inside each pita triangle.

5. Tear each **cheese slice** into 2 pieces. Stuff one piece of cheese into each pita triangle.

TiP

To make Pizza Stuffers in the microwave oven, follow steps 3 though 5 to make the stuffed pita triangles. Put the triangles on a microwave-safe plate and put the plate into the microwave. Heat on high for 30 seconds to 1 minute, or until the cheese has melted. Put on oven mitts and remove your Pizza Stuffers from the microwave. Let cool for 1 to 2 minutes before serving.

6. Put the stuffed pita triangles on the foil-covered toaster oven tray. Put on the oven mitts and put the tray back into the toaster oven.

7. Broil the Pizza Stuffers for 3 minutes, or until the cheese has melted. Watch carefully.

8. Wearing oven mitts, use the spatula to remove the Pizza Stuffers from the toaster oven and put them on the plate. (Be sure to turn off the toaster oven.) Let cool for 1 to 2 minutes before serving.

Invent-a-Recipe

What's a Sandangle? It's a pita triangle stuffed with anything you like! Just use your favorite combination of cheeses, beans, meats, vegetables, fruits, spreads, jellies, and jams in place of the sauce and cheese in this recipe. Eat your Sandangles cold, or heat them up like Pizza Stuffers.

Neato B'Nito

Makes 1 serving

Say Neato B'nito six times fast as you mash and squish the beans for this bean burrito!

Would you like to see how a bean starts growing? It's easy! First, wrap a small handful of dried beans (such as kidney beans or black beans) in a paper towel. Next, dampen the paper towel by pouring water over it. Put the wet paper towel in a plastic container. Dampen the towel once a day for the next couple of days. Your beans will begin to sprout in 1 to 3 days.

Ingredients

- 2 tablespoons salsa
- 1 soft tortilla
- $\frac{1}{3}$ cup canned black beans, drained
- 1 slice of your favorite cheese

Tools

- toaster oven
- foil
- measuring spoons
- table knife
- small, sturdy resealable plastic bag
- small spoon
- oven mitts
- timer
- metal spatula
- plate

1. Remove the tray from the toaster oven. Cover it with foil and set it aside.

2. Preheat the toaster oven to bake at 350°F.

3. Use the table knife to spread the **salsa** evenly over the **tortilla.**

4. Put the **black beans** into the plastic bag. Push the air out of the bag and seal it.

5. Use your fingers to mash and squish the beans until they are well squished. Squish as long as you like!

6. Spoon the squished beans onto the tortilla and spread evenly with the table knife.

7. Tear the **cheese** into small pieces and sprinkle it on top of the squished beans.

8. Roll the tortilla up so it looks like a burrito. Press on it gently with the palms of your hands to make it stay closed.

9. Put the tortilla on the foil-covered toaster oven tray. Put on oven mitts and put the toaster oven tray into the toaster oven.

10. Heat your Neato B'Nito for 7 minutes.

11. Wearing oven mitts, use the spatula to remove the Neato B'Nito from the toaster oven and put it on the plate. (Be sure to turn off the toaster oven.) Let cool for 1 to 2 minutes before serving.

TIP

To make a Neato B'Nito in the microwave oven, follow steps 3 through 8. Put your Neato B'Nito on a microwave-safe plate and put the plate in the microwave. Heat for 2 minutes on high. Wear oven mitts to remove your Neato B'Nito from the microwave. Let cool for 1 to 2 minutes before serving.

49

3

Sips, Dips, and Crisps

The recipes for these bubbly drinks, yummy dips, and irresistible munchies are all easy enough to make for after-school snacks, and so delicious that you'll want to serve them at your next party! Try the Invent-a-Recipe on page 59 and whip up your own awesome dip.

WHAT'S INSIDE:

- Cinnamon Apple Bubbles
- Purple Ginger Gulps
- Bubbling Yo-Yo
- Marvelous Maple Milk
- Sizzling Salsa
- Green Monster Mash
- Scrumptious Hummus
- Popcorn Honeys
- Garlic Crisps
- Chili Chip Strips
- Jack-O'-Lantern Seeds

Cinnamon Apple Bubbles

This apple juice soda is nice and spicy.

Makes I serving

Ingredients		Tools
I cranberry-apple tea bag	2 tablespoons frozen apple juice concentrate, thawed	large drinking glass
2 tablespoons water	I cup seltzer	measuring spoons
	2 shakes cinnamon	measuring cup
		spoon
		straw

1. Put the **tea bag** into the large glass. Add the **water** to the glass, pouring it over the tea bag.

2. When the water in the glass turns really red (after about I to 2 minutes), squeeze out the tea bag and remove it from the glass.

3. Add the **apple juice concentrate** to the glass.

4. Bubble it up by adding the **seltzer**.

5. Sprinkle with **cinnamon,** stir with the spoon, and sip with a straw.

Purple Ginger Gulps

This tangy grape and ginger soda bubbles all the way *down!*

Makes 1 serving

Does your stomach feel yucky and your face turn green during those really long car trips? Well, for your next long car trip, bring along some Purple Ginger Gulps! Ginger can help a carsick stomach feel much better.

Ingredients

3 tablespoons frozen grape juice concentrate, thawed

$\frac{1}{4}$ teaspoon powdered ginger

1 cup seltzer

Tools

measuring spoons

large drinking glass

small spoon

measuring cup

1. Put the **grape juice concentrate** and the **ginger** in the large glass. Stir well with the spoon.

2. Slowly pour in the **seltzer** and watch your Purple Ginger Gulps explode with purple bubbles!

3. Stir again and serve.

Bubbling Yo-Yo

This sensational bubbling yogurt shake will have you jumping up and down.

Makes 1 serving

Ingredients

2 tablespoons frozen orange juice concentrate, thawed

4 teaspoons frozen apple juice concentrate, thawed

2 tablespoons dried milk

$\frac{1}{3}$ cup plain yogurt

$\frac{1}{2}$ cup seltzer

Tools

measuring spoons

measuring cups

quart-sized plastic container with lid

large drinking glass

straw

1. Put the **orange juice concentrate, apple juice concentrate, dried milk, yogurt,** and **seltzer** into the plastic container. Seal tightly.

2. Holding your hand on the lid, shake the plastic container up and down as hard as you can. Jump up and down until everything is bubbling and well mixed together.

3. Pour your shake into the large glass and serve with a straw.

Marvelous Maple Milk

Here's a marvelous way to drink milk—straight from marvelous Maplewood, New Jersey.

Makes 1 serving

Milk, yogurt, and cheese are full of calcium—the mineral that makes your teeth and bones grow strong and hard. Your body also uses calcium to make your muscles work and to stop cuts from bleeding.

Your bones store calcium just as a bank stores money. When your body runs low on calcium, it withdraws the calcium from your bones. And when your body has enough calcium, it deposits it back into your bones so they can keep growing. So remember to invest in your bone bank by eating plenty of milk, yogurt, and cheese!

Ingredients	Tools	
1 cup milk	measuring cup	small spoon
1 tablespoon maple syrup	large drinking glass	straw
	measuring spoons	

1. Pour the **milk** into the large glass.

2. Add the **maple syrup,** stir with the spoon, and serve with a straw.

Sizzling Salsa

Makes about 1½ cups

Here's a spicy hot tomato dip for veggies and chips.

Ingredients

1 cup canned crushed tomatoes

½ cup canned corn, drained (or frozen corn, thawed)

1 green pepper

3 green onions (scallions)

¼ teaspoon garlic powder

1 tablespoon red vinegar

1 shake crushed hot red pepper

Tools

measuring cups

measuring spoons

medium mixing bowl

large spoon

plastic wrap

safety scissors

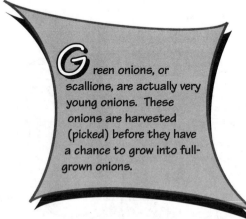

Green onions, or scallions, are actually very young onions. These onions are harvested (picked) before they have a chance to grow into full-grown onions.

1. Put the **crushed tomatoes** and **corn** into the mixing bowl. Use the large spoon to stir well.

2. Use your bare hands to tear the **green pepper** in half. Pull out the seeds and the white part of the pepper and throw them away.

3. Wrap one pepper half in plastic wrap and refrigerate. Set aside the other half.

4. Wash the safety scissors.

5. Use the scissors to cut the pepper half into little tiny pieces. Put the pepper pieces into the bowl.

6. Use the scissors to snip the **green onions** into tiny pieces and put them in the bowl. Snip both the green and the white part of the onion. (Throw out the roots.)

7. Add the **garlic powder, vinegar,** and **red pepper** to the bowl. Stir well with the spoon.

8. Serve your Sizzling Salsa with raw vegetables or tortilla chips.

Green Monster Mash

Make monster faces while you mash and squish this avocado dip!

Makes about 1½ cups

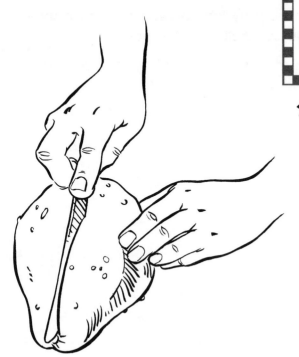

Ingredients	Tools	
1 ripe avocado	cutting board	large plastic bag
1 teaspoon lemon juice	table knife	measuring spoons
¼ cup salsa	medium mixing bowl	mixing spoon
¼ teaspoon salt		

1. Put the **avocado** on the cutting board. Use the table knife to cut the avocado in half, around the pit, from top to bottom. Split apart the two halves and remove the pit.

Invent-a-Recipe

What kind of dip do you like best? Spicy and hot? Smooth and creamy? Crunchy and chewy? Or cheesy and gooey? You can make a dip of your own. Just use combinations of fruits, vegetables, sauces, yogurt, cream cheese, cottage cheese, jelly, jam, mustard, ketchup, mayonnaise, and spices—you name it—in place of the ingredients in this recipe. Then dip in with vegetables, fruits, crackers, chips—whatever you'd like to use as dip sticks.

2. Peel off the avocado skin with your fingers and throw it away.

3. Use the table knife to cut the avocado into large chunks. Put the chunks in the bowl.

4. Put the plastic bag over your hand. Use your bagged hand to mash and squish the avocado until the avocado is super gooky.

5. Add the **lemon juice, salsa,** and **salt** to the bowl. Stir well with the spoon.

6. Scoop up your Green Monster Mash with vegetables or tortilla chips.

Scrumptious Hummus

This squishy chickpea dip is very popular in the Middle East.

Makes about 2 cups

Did you ever wonder how your insides get clean? Fiber! Fiber is the part of chickpeas, beans, fruits, vegetables, and whole grains that isn't digested (broken down) inside your body. Fiber cleans your stomach and carries out the waste your body doesn't need. Fiber is your body's janitor. Without it your body would be an awfully messy place!

Ingredients

- 1 15-ounce can chickpeas
- 1 tablespoon lemon juice
- 1 tablespoon water
- 3 tablespoons peanut butter or tahini (sesame butter)
- $\frac{1}{4}$ teaspoon garlic powder
- 2 shakes salt

Tools

- can opener
- colander
- large spoon
- 1-gallon sturdy resealable plastic bag
- medium mixing bowl
- measuring spoons

1. Use the can opener to open the can of **chickpeas.** Put the colander in the sink and put the chickpeas in the colander to drain off the liquid.

2. Use the large spoon to put the chickpeas in the plastic bag. Push the air out of the bag and seal it.

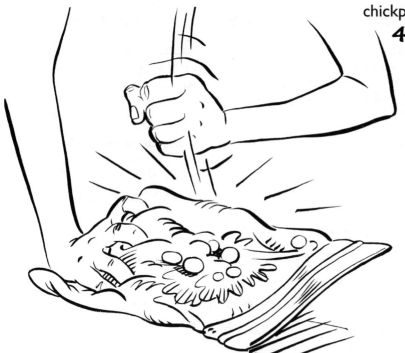

3. Pound, mash, and squish the bag with your hands and fingers until the chickpeas are well squished. Spoon the squished chickpeas into the bowl.

4. Add the **lemon juice, water, peanut butter, garlic powder,** and **salt** to the bowl. Stir well with the spoon.

5. Serve your Scrumptious Hummus with toasted pita bread.

Popcorn Honeys

Share this sweet and sticky popcorn with a special friend.

Makes 4 to 6 servings

Ingredients

4 cups air-popped popcorn (store-bought or homemade)

1 tablespoon vegetable oil

2 tablespoons honey

3 tablespoons shelled peanuts

Tools

measuring cup

large mixing bowl

measuring spoons

small spoon

small, sturdy resealable plastic bag

rolling pin

1. Put the **popcorn** in the bowl.

2. Put the **oil** and the **honey** in a measuring cup. Use the spoon to stir well.

3. Pour the oil-honey mixture over the popcorn.

4. Put the **peanuts** in the plastic bag. Push the air out of the bag and seal it.

Have you ever wondered why popcorn pops? Inside each unpopped popcorn kernel is a tiny bit of water. When the kernel is heated, the water inside the kernel boils. The boiling water turns into steam, and the steam pops the kernel.

5. Use the rolling pin to bash and smash the peanuts until they are well smashed.

6. Pour the smashed peanuts over the popcorn. Use your hands to mix well, and serve.

Garlic Crisps

Makes 2 servings

Here's a simple recipe for skinny crisps of garlic bread.

Ingredients	Tools	
1 tablespoon margarine	toaster oven	table knife
$\frac{1}{4}$ teaspoon garlic powder	foil	oven mitts
$\frac{1}{4}$ teaspoon paprika	measuring spoons	timer
1 pita bread	small mixing bowl	spatula
	small spoon	plate
	cutting board	

1. Remove the tray from the toaster oven. Cover it with foil and set aside.

2. Preheat the toaster oven to medium broil.

3. Put the **margarine, garlic powder,** and **paprika** in the bowl. Mix well with the spoon.

4. Put the **pita bread** on the cutting board. Use the table knife to cut the pita in half. Cut each half in half to make 4 triangles.

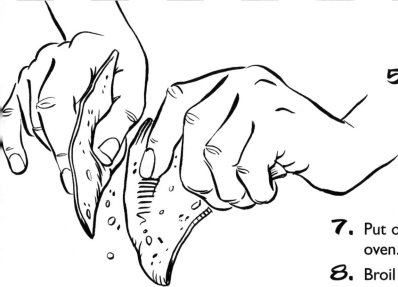

5. Open each pita triangle and tear it at the fold to make 2 more triangles. You should have 8 triangles.

6. Use the table knife to spread a little bit of the garlic margarine mixture on each triangle. Put the pita triangles on the foil-covered toaster oven tray.

7. Put on oven mitts and put the tray back in the toaster oven.

8. Broil the Garlic Crisps for 1 to 2 minutes. Watch carefully, these burn easily!

9. Wearing oven mitts, use the spatula to remove the Garlic Crisps from the toaster oven and put them on the plate. (Be sure to turn off the toaster oven.)

10. Serve these Garlic Crisps hot!

Chili Chip Strips

You'll flip for these spicy chip strips!

Makes 2 servings

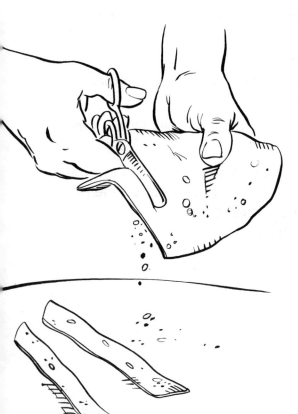

Ingredients	Tools	
1 tablespoon vegetable oil	toaster oven	small spoon
1 tablespoon grated Parmesan cheese	foil	safety scissors
1 teaspoon chili powder	measuring spoons	oven mitts
$\frac{1}{4}$ teaspoon salt	medium mixing bowl	timer
3 small soft corn tortillas		

1. Remove the tray from the toaster oven. Cover it with foil and set aside.

2. Preheat the toaster oven to medium broil.

3. Put the **oil, Parmesan cheese, chili powder,** and **salt** into the bowl. Stir well with the spoon.

4. Wash and dry the safety scissors.

5. Fold each **tortilla** in half. Use the scissors to cut each folded tortilla into 4 or 5 strips. Put the tortilla strips in the bowl.

6. Use your hands to toss the strips with the oil-spice mixture. Be sure to coat all of the strips with the mixture.

7. Put the tortilla strips on the foil-covered tray.

8. Put on the oven mitts and put the tray back in the toaster oven.

9. Broil the tortilla strips for 4 minutes. Watch carefully— these burn easily.

10. Wearing oven mitts, remove the tray from the toaster oven. Put the tray on top of the toaster oven, or on the stove. (Be sure to turn off the toaster oven.) Let cool for 5 minutes before serving.

Jack-O'-Lantern Seeds

Share these crunchy pumpkin seeds with a friendly goblin.

Makes 2 to 4 servings

Ingredients	Tools	
2 cups washed and dried pumpkin seeds	measuring cup	cookie sheet
1 tablespoon vegetable oil	measuring spoons	oven mitts
1 teaspoon salt	medium mixing bowl	adult helper
	large spoon	

1. Preheat the oven to 300°F.

2. Put the **pumpkin seeds** in the bowl.

3. Add the **oil** and the **salt.** Use the spoon or your hands to mix well.

4. Pour the oiled pumpkin seeds onto the cookie sheet. Use your hands to spread the seeds evenly over the cookie sheet.

TIP

Use the seeds from your Halloween pumpkin to make your jack-o'-lantern seeds. Ask an adult to cut the pumpkin open. Scoop out all the seeds with a spoon. Then use your fingers to remove the gooky, slimy fibers from the seeds. Put the seeds in a colander and rinse with cold water until clean. Pat the seeds dry with a cloth or paper towel, and store in a plastic container until you're ready to use them.

5. Have your adult helper place the cookie sheet in the oven. Bake for 35 minutes.

6. Have your adult helper remove the seeds from the oven. Let cool for 5 minutes before serving.

Side Dish Funnies

This chapter is stuffed with fun and tasty side dish recipes. You'll find easy-to-make dressings and salads at the beginning and middle of the chapter. The more challenging recipes for potatoes and rice are at the end of the chapter. And you can invent your own Super Salad with the Invent-a-Recipe on page 77.

WHAT'S INSIDE:

- Garlic Parmesan Dressing
- Orange Honey Dressing
- Applenut Hunker Chunks
- Veggie Mix-Up
- Salad Kabobs
- Bird's Nest Salad
- Crouton Crunchers
- Smashed Potato Cakes
- Potato Stuffers
- House Special Fried Rice

Garlic Parmesan Dressing

You'll jump up and down—really!—to make this tasty salad dressing.

Makes about $\frac{3}{4}$ cup

Ingredients

$\frac{1}{2}$ cup red vinegar

$\frac{1}{4}$ cup water

1 teaspoon basil

1 teaspoon oregano

1 teaspoon garlic powder

2 tablespoons grated Parmesan cheese

2 tablespoons vegetable oil

Tools

measuring cups

measuring spoons

1-quart plastic container with lid

funnel

plastic squeeze bottle or empty salad dressing bottle

1. Put the **vinegar, water, basil, oregano, garlic powder, Parmesan cheese,** and **oil** into the plastic container and seal tightly.

2. Hold your hand on the lid of the container and shake the container up and down as hard as you can. Jump around the kitchen until the ingredients are well mixed together.

3. Fit the funnel into the top of the bottle. Carefully pour the salad dressing through the funnel into the bottle.

4. Serve your Garlic Parmesan Dressing on top of your favorite salad.

Orange Honey Dressing

Here's another jumping salad dressing—this one's tangy-sweet.

Makes about $\frac{1}{2}$ cup

In 1912 a British explorer named Robert Falcon Scott and his crew hiked off to explore the South Pole. They never returned. They all died of a deadly disease called scurvy. Believe it or not, a few oranges, lemons, or limes would have saved them! Oranges are chock-full of vitamin C, the vitamin that prevents scurvy and keeps your gums and skin healthy.

Ingredients

3 tablespoons red wine vinegar

3 tablespoons frozen orange juice concentrate, thawed

3 tablespoons vegetable oil

3 tablespoons honey

1 teaspoon mustard

1 teaspoon salt

Tools

measuring spoons

1-quart plastic container with lid

funnel

plastic squeeze bottle or empty salad dressing bottle

1. Put the **vinegar, orange juice concentrate, oil, honey, mustard,** and **salt** in the plastic container and seal tightly.

2. Put your hand on the lid of the container and shake the container up and down as hard as you can. Jump up and down! Dance around! Shake until all the ingredients are well mixed together.

3. Fit the funnel into the squeeze bottle. Carefully pour the dressing through the funnel into the bottle.

4. Serve this dressing on top of your next batch of Super Salad (see page 77).

73

Applenut Hunker Chunks

Munch a bunch of this sweet and crunchy apple-nut salad.

Makes 2 servings

In the early 1800s there lived a preacher named John Chapman. Wearing tattered clothes, and with a pot on top of his head, he wandered far and wide, collecting the apple seeds thrown out by the workers at cider mills. Mr. Chapman planted these seeds up and down the Ohio Valley, and they turned into apple orchards. The people gave him a nickname: Johnny Appleseed.

Ingredients

- 1 large apple
- 2 tablespoons raisins
- 2 tablespoons chopped nuts, such as walnuts or almonds
- $\frac{1}{4}$ cup plain yogurt
- 2 teaspoons honey or sugar
- sprinkle of cinnamon

Tools

cutting board
table knife
small mixing bowl
measuring spoons
large spoon
measuring cup

---

1. Put the **apple** on the cutting board. Hold the apple down with one hand while you stick the tip of the table knife into the top of the apple. Pull the knife out and cut the apple from top to bottom where you made the cut.

2. Repeat step 1 until you've cut the whole apple into big pieces.

3. Remove the seeds from the apple pieces.

4. Use the table knife to cut the apple pieces into chunks the size of game dice. Put the apple chunks in the mixing bowl.

5. Add the **raisins** and the **nuts** to the bowl. Stir with the large spoon.

6. Put the **yogurt, honey,** and **cinnamon** into the measuring cup. Stir well.

7. Pour the yogurt mixture into the mixing bowl, stir again, and serve.

Veggie Mix-Up

Here's a jumping-up-and-down way to make a colorful salad.

Makes 2 servings

Ingredients

4 cherry tomatoes
½ cucumber
½ cup canned red or black beans, drained
½ cup canned or frozen corn, thawed
1 tablespoon of your favorite salad dressing
1 tablespoon grated Parmesan cheese

Tools

cutting board
table knife
1-quart plastic container with lid
vegetable peeler
measuring cups
measuring spoons

1. Put the **tomatoes** on the cutting board. Stick the tip of the table knife into a tomato. Pull out the knife and cut the tomato in half where you made the cut.

2. Cut the tomato halves in half. Put the tomato pieces in the plastic container.

3. Repeat steps 1 and 2 with the rest of the tomatoes.

4. Put the **cucumber** on the cutting board. Use the vegetable peeler to peel the cucumber.

5. Use the table knife to cut the peeled cucumber in half, the long way. Cut the cucumber halves into long strips. Then cut the cucumber strips into pieces the size of game dice. Put the pieces in the plastic container.

6. Add the **beans, corn, salad dressing,** and **Parmesan cheese** to the container, and seal tightly.

7. Put your hand on the lid of the container and shake the container up and down until your Veggie Mix-Up is well mixed together. Jump around the kitchen while you do this!

8. Serve your Veggie Mix-Up right away.

Invent·a·Recipe

Super Salads can be crunchy, munchy, sticky, or chewy. They can be sweet, sour, warm, or cool. It's up to you. Instead of the ingredients in this recipe, just use combinations of your favorite fruits, vegetables, cheeses, beans, meats, crunchies, salad dressings, and anything else you would love to put in a salad.

Salad Kabobs

Makes 1 serving

Here's a funny way to eat a cucumber and lettuce salad.

Ingredients	Tools
2 or 3 large lettuce leaves	cutting board
$\frac{1}{2}$ cucumber	vegetable peeler
1 tablespoon salad dressing	table knife
	1 chopstick
	measuring spoons

1. Tear each **lettuce leaf** into 2 or 3 pieces. Set aside.

2. Put the **cucumber** on the cutting board. Use the vegetable peeler to peel the cucumber.

3. Use the table knife to cut the cucumber into 5 or 6 slices.

4. Slide a piece of lettuce onto the chopstick. Next, slide a cucumber slice onto the chopstick.

5. Continue sliding lettuce and cucumber slices onto the chopstick until you've used all of the lettuce and cucumber pieces.

6. Dribble the **salad dressing** on your Salad Kabob and eat it like corn-on-the-cob. Enjoy!

Bird's Nest Salad

Makes 2 to 4 servings

Turn on a bright light in a dark room. Then quickly turn off the light. How long does it take before you can see clearly again? If you are "blind" for more than a couple of seconds, eat some carrots! Why? Carrots are full of beta carotene, which your body turns into vitamin A. Vitamin A sends a signal to your brain so that you can see again after a flash of light at night. So, eat some carrots and give your eyes a flashlight at night!

Here's a quick and crunchy carrot salad.

Ingredients	Tools	
2 carrots	cutting board	measuring spoons
2 tablespoons raisins	vegetable peeler	measuring cup
2 tablespoons yogurt	grater	small spoon
1 teaspoon honey	small mixing bowl	plate

1. Use the peeler to peel the **carrot** on the cutting board.

2. Use the grater to shred the carrots on the cutting board. Put the shredded carrots in the bowl.

3. Add the **raisins** to the bowl. Mix well with the spoon.

4. Put the **yogurt** into the measuring cup. Add the **honey** and stir well.

5. Pour the yogurt-honey mixture onto the carrot mixture. Mix thoroughly with the spoon.

6. Put some of the salad onto a plate and shape into a bird's nest. Enjoy!

Crouton Crunchers

These crispy, crunchy croutons will cheer up any soup or salad.

Makes 2 to 4 servings

Ingredients

1 teaspoon margarine
1 tablespoon oil
1 tablespoon vinegar
2 tablespoons grated Parmesan cheese
$\frac{1}{4}$ teaspoon salt
$\frac{1}{4}$ teaspoon garlic or onion powder
$\frac{1}{4}$ teaspoon basil
2 slices bread

Tools

measuring spoons
small piece of waxed paper
cookie sheet
medium mixing bowl
small spoon
table knife
cutting board
oven mitts
timer
adult helper

---

1. Preheat the oven to 300°F.

2. Use the waxed paper and the **margarine** to grease the cookie sheet.

3. Put the **oil, vinegar, Parmesan cheese, salt, garlic powder,** and **basil** into the mixing bowl. Stir with the spoon.

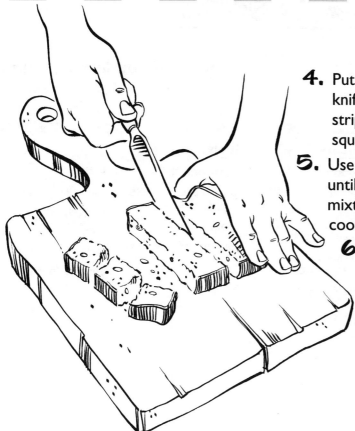

4. Put the **bread** on the cutting board. Use the table knife to cut the bread into 3 strips. Next, cut the strips into 4 or 5 small squares. Put the bread squares into the bowl.

5. Use your fingers to gently toss the bread squares until they are all well coated with the oil-vinegar mixture. Put the coated bread squares on the cookie sheet.

6. Ask your adult helper to place the cookie sheet in the oven. Bake for 25 minutes.

7. Have the adult remove the croutons from the oven. Let cool for 5 minutes.

8. Sprinkle your Crouton Crunchers in your favorite soup or salad.

Smashed Potato Cakes

Here's a scrumptious way to use up leftover mashed potatoes.

Makes about 12 potato cakes (2 to 4 servings)

Ingredients	Tools	
1 teaspoon margarine	measuring spoons	fork
1 egg	small piece of waxed paper	measuring cups
2 cups leftover mashed potatoes	cookie sheet	large spoon
$\frac{1}{4}$ cup grated Parmesan cheese	medium mixing bowl	oven mitts
$\frac{1}{4}$ teaspoon garlic or onion powder		timer
$\frac{1}{4}$ teaspoon salt		adult helper
1 shake pepper		
2 slices bread		

1. Preheat the oven to 350°F.

2. Use the waxed paper and **margarine** to grease the cookie sheet.

3. Carefully crack the **egg** into the mixing bowl. Use the fork to mix well.

4. Add the **mashed potatoes, Parmesan cheese, garlic powder, salt,** and **pepper** to the bowl. Stir well with the spoon.

5. Use your fingers to crumble up each slice of **bread** into small crumbs. Add the crumbs to the bowl. Stir well.

6. Take some of the potato mixture and shape it into a ball about the size of a golf ball. Flatten the ball into a small pancake and put it on the greased cookie sheet.

7. Repeat step 6 until you've used up all of the potato mixture, placing the potato cakes 1 to 2 inches apart on the cookie sheet.

8. Ask your adult helper to put the cookie sheet in the oven. Bake the potato cakes for 25 minutes.

9. Have the adult remove the potato cakes from the oven. Let cool for 2 to 3 minutes before serving.

Potato Stuffers

Makes 8 servings

Thousands of years ago, the Native Americans who lived in the Andes Mountains in South America grew lots of potatoes. To prevent the potatoes from spoiling, they froze them outside at night. The next day they mashed and smashed the frozen potatoes. All this mashing and smashing dried out the potatoes and kept them from spoiling. The dried potatoes were called chuno.

These stuffed baked potatoes are good stuff.

Ingredients

2 or 3 slices cheese, such as cheddar or American

$\frac{1}{2}$ cup cottage cheese

$\frac{1}{4}$ teaspoon garlic powder

2 shakes paprika

2 green onions (scallions)

4 cooled baked potatoes

Tools

medium mixing bowl

measuring cup

measuring spoons

small spoon

safety scissors

cutting board

table knife

large plastic bag

cookie sheet

oven mitts

timer

adult helper

1. Preheat the oven to 350°F.

2. Tear the **cheese** into little pieces. Put the cheese pieces in the bowl.

3. Add the **cottage cheese, garlic powder,** and **paprika** to the bowl. Use the spoon to stir well.

4. Wash the safety scissors.

5. Use scissors to snip the **green onions** into little pieces. Snip both the green and the white part of the onion. (Throw away the roots.) Put the pieces in the bowl and stir well.

6. Put the **potatoes** on the cutting board and use the table knife to cut them in half the long way.

7. Using the point of the spoon, scoop out most of the white part of each potato half and put it in the bowl with the cheese mixture. Be careful not to break the potato skins.

8. Put the plastic bag over your hand. Use your bagged hand to squish the potato-cheese mixture together until well smushed.

9. Use the spoon to stuff about 2 or 3 spoonfuls of the smushed mixture back into each potato skin. Put the stuffed potatoes on the cookie sheet.

10. Ask your adult helper to put the cookie sheet in the oven. Bake the Potato Stuffers for 5 to 10 minutes, or until the stuffing is browned.

11. Have the adult remove the potatoes from the oven. Let cool for 2 to 3 minutes before serving.

TiP

If you don't have any leftover baked potatoes, ask an adult to help you make them. It's best to use long, oval-shaped Russet potatoes to make baked potatoes. First, preheat the oven to 400°F. Wash and dry the potatoes. Use a fork to pierce each potato in 3 or 4 places. Bake them directly on the oven racks for 45 to 60 minutes, depending on size.

House Special Fried Rice

Flavorful vegetables and soy sauce give this dish its very special taste.

Makes 4 servings

Ingredients	**Tools**	
1 celery stalk	table knife	wooden spoon
2 green onions (scallions)	cutting board	skillet
$\frac{1}{2}$ cup mixed frozen peas and carrots, thawed	large mixing bowl	oven mitts
	safety scissors	timer
10 white mushrooms	measuring cups	adult helper
2 tablespoons soy sauce	measuring spoons	
2 tablespoons vegetable oil		
$2\frac{1}{2}$ cups cooked rice, brown or white		

1. Put the **celery** on the cutting board and use the table knife to cut it down the middle, the long way.

2. Cut or break the celery halves into little pieces. Put the pieces in the mixing bowl.

3. Wash the safety scissors.

4. Use the scissors to snip the **green onions** into tiny pieces. Snip both the green and the white part of the onion. (Throw away the roots.) Put the pieces in the bowl.

5. Add the **peas** and **carrots** to the bowl.

6. Use your fingers to break the **mushrooms** into little pieces. Add the mushroom pieces to the bowl.

7. Add the **soy sauce, oil,** and **rice.** Stir well with the wooden spoon.

8. Have your adult helper heat the skillet on the stove for 30 seconds over medium heat.

9. Add the rice mixture to the skillet. With the adult's help, cook for 7 minutes, stirring constantly with the wooden spoon. Let cool for 1 to 2 minutes before serving.

TiP

If you don't have any leftover cooked brown rice, ask an adult to help you make some. To make about 3 cups of cooked brown rice, first boil $2\frac{1}{4}$ cups water and $\frac{1}{2}$ teaspoon salt in a heavy-bottomed pot. Slowly add 1 cup dry rice to the boiling water. Return to a boil, then cover. Simmer over low heat for 40 to 45 minutes, or until the water has been absorbed.

5

Supper Stuff

The dinner recipes in this chapter are kid-approved and they're guaranteed to taste good! All of the Supper Stuff recipes are fun to make in the usual Mash and Smash way. However, all of these recipes are three-hand recipes and require the use of the oven or stove, so be sure to ask an adult to help! For extra fun, try the Casserole Surprise Invent-a-Recipe on page 97.

What's Inside:

▸ Spaghetti Soup
▸ Smash and Squish
  Spaghetti Sauce
▸ Easy Cheesy Baked Shells
▸ Three-Tortilla Pie
▸ Tom's Teriyaki Chicken
▸ Crispy Orange Chicken
▸ Awesome Peanut Butter Noodles

Spaghetti Soup

Spaghetti and mixed vegetables make this a super supper soup.

Makes 6 to 8 servings

Ingredients		Tools
3 garlic cloves, peeled	1 teaspoon salt	small, sturdy resealable plastic bag
2 tablespoons vegetable oil	$\frac{1}{4}$ teaspoon oregano	rolling pin
1 bunch green onions (scallions)	$\frac{1}{4}$ teaspoon basil	small spoon
1 28-ounce can crushed tomatoes	4 cups water	large, heavy-bottomed soup pot
1 12-ounce bag mixed frozen vegetables	$\frac{1}{2}$ pound dry spaghetti	measuring spoons
	grated Parmesan cheese	measuring cups
		safety scissors
		wooden spoon
		can opener
		timer
		oven mitts
		adult helper

> **TIP**
> To peel a clove of garlic, put it on a cutting board. Then use the bottom of a juice glass to gently smash the garlic. Use your fingers to peel off the dry, crackly skin.

1. Put the peeled **garlic cloves** in the plastic bag. Push the air out of the bag and seal.

2. Use the rolling pin to pound and smash the garlic until it is well mashed. Spoon the smashed garlic into the soup pot.

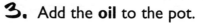

3. Add the **oil** to the pot.

4. Wash the safety scissors.

5. Use the scissors to snip the **green onions** into tiny pieces. Snip both the green and the white part of the onion. (Throw away the roots.) Put the onion pieces in the soup pot.

6. Ask your adult helper to cook the garlic, oil, and green onions for 1 minute over medium heat, stirring constantly with the wooden spoon. Have the adult remove the pot from the heat.

7. Use the can opener to open the **crushed tomatoes** and add them to the pot.

8. Add the **mixed vegetables, salt, oregano, basil,** and **water** to the pot. Stir well with the wooden spoon.

9. Hold about 10 pieces of **spaghetti** over the soup pot and break them into small pieces, about 1 to 2 inches long.

10. Repeat step 9 until you've broken all the spaghetti into the pot.

11. Have your adult helper help you cook the soup over medium heat for 30 minutes. Stir often.

12. Sprinkle about 1 tablespoon of **Parmesan cheese** over each serving of Spaghetti Soup.

Smash and Squish Spaghetti Sauce

You'll smash, bash, pound, and squish to make this delicious sauce.

Makes about 4 cups sauce

Ingredients	Tools	
3 cloves garlic, peeled	small, sturdy resealable plastic bag	wooden spoon
1 tablespoon vegetable oil	rolling pin	can opener
1 28-ounce can whole peeled tomatoes	3-quart heavy-bottomed pot with lid	large mixing bowl
2 6-ounce cans tomato paste	small spoon	large plastic bag
2 teaspoons dried oregano	measuring spoons	oven mitts
2 teaspoons dried basil		timer
1 teaspoon salt		adult helper
$1\frac{1}{2}$ cups water		

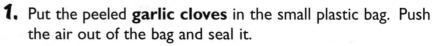

1. Put the peeled **garlic cloves** in the small plastic bag. Push the air out of the bag and seal it.

2. Use the rolling pin to pound, bash, and smash the garlic until it is well mashed. Spoon the smashed garlic into the pot.

Spice up your sauce by adding 1 to 2 cups of any of the following:
- Chopped red or green peppers (Cook these with the oil and garlic.)
- Chopped onions (Cook these with the oil and garlic.)
- Sliced mushrooms (Cook these with the oil and garlic.)
- Cooked ground beef or turkey (Stir this in at the end of the cooking time.)

A tomato is a vegetable, right? Wrong. A tomato is a fruit. A fruit is a yummy package of juice, seeds, and pulp, all wrapped up in a layer of skin. Because the tomato is not very sweet, many people think it's a vegetable. Back in the sixteenth century, however, people in England knew the tomato was a fruit. They called it the Love Apple!

3. Add the **oil** to the pot.

4. Have your adult helper cook the garlic and oil on the stove over medium heat for 1 minute, stirring constantly with the wooden spoon. Have the adult remove the pot from the heat.

5. Use the can opener to open the **whole tomatoes** and the **tomato paste.** Put the whole tomatoes and their liquid in the bowl. Set aside the tomato paste.

6. Put the large plastic bag over your hand. Use your bagged hand to squish the tomatoes until they are well squished. Really dig in and squish!

7. Use the small spoon to put the tomato paste in the bowl with the squished tomatoes. Stir well with the wooden spoon. (Be sure to scrape any tomato paste off the sides of the bowl.)

8. Pour the tomato mixture into the pot. Add the **oregano, basil, salt**, and **water.** Stir well.

9. Ask your adult helper to help you cook the sauce, partially covered, over medium heat for about an hour. Stir often with the wooden spoon, being sure to always wear oven mitts. (The sauce will splatter!)

10. Serve your Smash and Squish Spaghetti Sauce on top of your favorite pasta.

Easy Cheesy Baked Shells

Makes 4 servings

These tasty, chewy, cheesy shells are truly easy to make!

It takes 8 to 10 pounds of milk to make 1 pound of cheese!

Ingredients

- 1 teaspoon margarine
- 2½ cups dry small pasta shells
- ½ pound sliced Muenster cheese
- 3 cups milk
- 2 tablespoons cornstarch
- 1 teaspoon salt
- 1 teaspoon vegetable oil
- 1 teaspoon mustard
- 4 shakes paprika
- 1 slice of bread

Tools

- measuring spoons
- small piece of waxed paper
- 2- or 3-quart baking dish
- measuring cups
- small bowl
- 3-quart heavy-bottomed pot
- wire whisk
- wooden spoon
- oven mitts
- timer
- adult helper

1. Preheat the oven to 350°F.

2. Use the waxed paper and the **margarine** to grease the baking dish.

3. Pour the **pasta shells** into the baking dish, and set aside.

4. Break all of the **Muenster cheese** into small pieces, and put the pieces in the bowl.

5. Pour the **milk** into the 3-quart pot. Add the **cornstarch.** Use the wire whisk to mix well.

6. Add the **salt, oil, mustard,** and **paprika** to the milk mixture in the pot. Mix well with the wire whisk.

7. Have your adult helper help you heat the milk mixture over medium heat for 6 to 7 minutes, or until it thickens, stirring constantly with the wooden spoon. Have the adult remove the pot from the heat.

8. Add the cheese pieces to the milk mixture. Use the wooden spoon to stir the mixture until the cheese melts.

9. Have your adult helper pour the cheese sauce over the pasta shells in the baking dish. Use the wooden spoon to carefully stir the shells and the sauce until they are well mixed together.

10. With your fingers, crumble the **bread** into tiny pieces. Sprinkle the bread pieces on top of the pasta shells.

11. Have the adult put the baking dish in the oven. Bake for 35 minutes.

12. Have the adult remove the shells from the oven. Let cool for 5 to 10 minutes.

13. Serve your Easy Cheesy Baked Shells next to an easy green salad.

Three-Tortilla Pie

Beans, peppers, salsa, and cheese make this one great tortilla pie.

Makes 4 servings

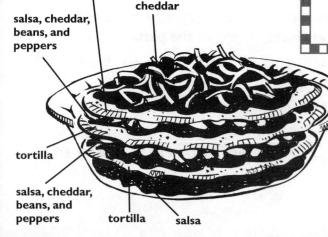

tortilla

salsa and cheddar

salsa, cheddar, beans, and peppers

tortilla

salsa, cheddar, beans, and peppers

tortilla

salsa

Ingredients

1 to 2 teaspoons margarine

$1\frac{1}{2}$ cups shredded cheddar cheese

1 cup canned beans, such as black, pinto, or red beans, drained

1 cup frozen chopped red peppers or corn, thawed

$\frac{1}{2}$ cup salsa

3 soft tortillas

Tools

measuring spoons

small piece of waxed paper

pie pan

measuring cups

grater

cutting board

medium mixing bowl

large spoon

small bowl

oven mitts

timer

adult helper

---

1. Preheat the oven to 350°F.

2. Use the waxed paper and **margarine** to grease the pie pan. Set aside.

3. Use the grater to shred the **cheddar cheese** on the cutting board. Set aside.

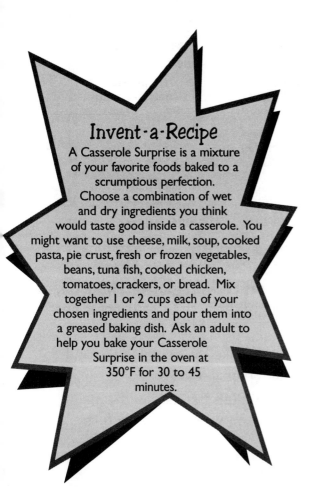

Invent-a-Recipe

A Casserole Surprise is a mixture of your favorite foods baked to a scrumptious perfection. Choose a combination of wet and dry ingredients you think would taste good inside a casserole. You might want to use cheese, milk, soup, cooked pasta, pie crust, fresh or frozen vegetables, beans, tuna fish, cooked chicken, tomatoes, crackers, or bread. Mix together 1 or 2 cups each of your chosen ingredients and pour them into a greased baking dish. Ask an adult to help you bake your Casserole Surprise in the oven at 350°F for 30 to 45 minutes.

4. Put the **beans** and **peppers** (or **corn**) in the mixing bowl. Use the large spoon to mix well. Set aside.

5. Put 2 tablespoons of the **salsa** in the greased pie pan. Spread it evenly over the bottom of the pan with the large spoon.

6. Put one **tortilla** on top of the salsa. Cover it with 2 tablespoons of salsa, half of the bean and pepper (or corn) mixture from the bowl, and $\frac{1}{2}$ cup of the grated cheddar. As you add each ingredient, use the large spoon to spread it evenly over the tortilla.

7. Put the second tortilla on top of the shredded cheese. Add 2 tablespoons of the salsa, then the remaining bean and pepper mixture, then $\frac{1}{2}$ cup of the cheddar cheese. Spread each ingredient with the large spoon.

8. Top with the third tortilla. Add the remaining salsa, then the remaining cheddar cheese, spreading each with the spoon.

9. Ask your adult helper to place the pie pan in the oven. Bake for 25 minutes.

10. Ask the adult to remove the Three-Tortilla Pie from the oven. Let cool for 5 minutes, then serve.

Tom's Teriyaki Chicken

Makes 4 servings

This tangy dish is sure to be a family favorite!

Ingredients

$\frac{1}{4}$ cup sesame seeds

$\frac{1}{4}$ cup soy sauce

$\frac{1}{4}$ cup vinegar

$\frac{1}{4}$ cup ketchup

2 tablespoons vegetable oil

2 tablespoons honey

$\frac{1}{4}$ teaspoon garlic or onion powder

$\frac{1}{4}$ teaspoon powdered ginger (optional)

1 pound boneless, skinless chicken breasts

Tools

measuring cups

measuring spoons

2-quart plastic container with lid

large spoon

timer

fork

broiler pan

oven mitts

adult helper

1. Put the **sesame seeds, soy sauce, vinegar, ketchup, oil, honey, garlic powder,** and **ginger** in the plastic container. Seal tightly.

2. Hold your hand on the lid and shake the container up and down as hard as you can. Jump up and down!

3. Use your fingers to put the **chicken breasts** in the container with the sauce. Use the spoon to gently turn

Remember to wash your hands well with soap and water after touching raw chicken.

the chicken breasts in the sauce until they are completely covered with sauce.

4. Put the lid back on the container and put it in the refrigerator for 30 minutes.

5. Preheat the broiler of the oven to medium high.

6. After 30 minutes, use the fork to remove the chicken breasts from the container and put them on the broiler pan.

7. Have your adult helper put the broiler pan in the oven. Broil the chicken for 15 to 20 minutes.

8. Ask the adult to help you check the chicken for doneness and to remove the chicken when it's finished.

9. Serve Tom's Teriyaki Chicken hot with rice and a dark green vegetable.

Crispy Orange Chicken

This crispy oven-baked chicken is great picnic food.

Makes 4 servings

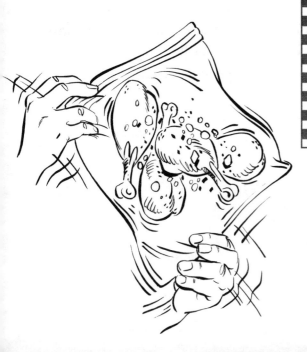

Ingredients

1 teaspoon margarine

7 saltine crackers

2 tablespoons cornmeal

2 tablespoons wheat germ

3 tablespoons grated Parmesan cheese

$\frac{1}{2}$ teaspoon salt

$\frac{1}{4}$ teaspoon basil

$\frac{1}{4}$ teaspoon oregano

$\frac{1}{4}$ teaspoon onion or garlic powder

2 tablespoons frozen orange juice concentrate, thawed

1 tablespoon vegetable oil

3 tablespoons honey

4 to 6 pieces chicken, such as drumsticks, legs, thighs, or boneless breasts

Tools

measuring spoons

small piece of waxed paper

cookie sheet

1-gallon sturdy resealable plastic bag

large mixing bowl

large spoon

oven mitts

timer

adult helper

1. Preheat the oven to 350°F.

2. Use the waxed paper and **margarine** to grease the cookie sheet. Set aside.

3. Put the **crackers, cornmeal, wheat germ, Parmesan cheese, salt, basil, oregano,** and **onion powder** in the plastic bag. Push the air out of the bag and seal it.

4. Pound and smash the bag with your fists until the crackers are all smashed up. Then shake the bag up and down to mix the ingredients together.

5. Put the **orange juice concentrate, oil,** and **honey** in the mixing bowl. Stir well with the large spoon.

6. Put the **chicken pieces** in the bowl. Use the wooden spoon to stir the chicken with the orange-honey sauce until each piece is completely coated with sauce.

7. Use your fingers to put the chicken pieces into the bag with the cracker crumb mixture. Push the air out of the bag and seal it.

8. Shake the bag up and down and all around until the chicken pieces are covered with the cracker-crumb mixture.

9. Use your fingers to put the chicken pieces on the cookie sheet. Arrange them so that none are touching. (Throw away the plastic bag when you're finished.)

10. Have your adult helper put the chicken in the oven and bake it for 20 to 45 minutes.

11. Ask the adult to check the chicken for doneness and to remove it from the oven when finished. Let cool for 5 minutes.

12. You can serve your Crispy Orange Chicken hot or cold.

TiP

Remember to wash your hands well with soap and water after touching raw chicken.

TiP

Boneless chicken breasts usually take about 20 minutes to cook. Chicken legs, thighs, and drumsticks usually take 35 to 45 minutes, depending upon size.

101

Awesome Peanut Butter Noodles

Makes 4 servings

These sweet and spicy noodles are delicious!

Ingredients

- $\frac{1}{2}$ cup unsweetened peanut butter
- $\frac{1}{4}$ cup red wine vinegar
- $\frac{1}{4}$ cup soy sauce
- $\frac{1}{2}$ cup water
- 3 tablespoons sugar
- 2 cloves garlic, peeled
- 2 cups frozen green vegetables, such as chopped broccoli or peas, thawed
- 4 cups cooked pasta, such as spaghetti or spirals

Tools

- measuring cups
- measuring spoons
- medium mixing bowl
- large spoon
- small, sturdy resealable plastic bag
- rolling pin
- small spoon
- large skillet
- wooden spoon
- oven mitts
- adult helper

1. Put the **peanut butter, red vinegar, soy sauce, water,** and **sugar** in the mixing bowl. Stir well with the large spoon until all of the lumps of peanut butter are broken up.

2. Put the peeled **garlic cloves** into the plastic bag. Push the air out of the bag and seal it.

102

3. Use the rolling pin to bash and smash the garlic until it is well smashed.

4. Use the small spoon to add the smashed garlic to the mixing bowl. Stir well with the large spoon.

5. Pour the peanut butter mixture into the skillet. Have your adult helper cook it on the stove for 1 minute over medium heat, stirring constantly with the wooden spoon.

6. Add the thawed frozen **green vegetables** and the **cooked pasta** to the skillet. Cook, stirring constantly, for 3 to 5 more minutes.

7. Have the adult remove the skillet from the heat.

8. Slurp up your Awesome Peanut Butter Noodles right away!

TIP

If you don't have any leftover cooked pasta, ask an adult to help you make some. Use $\frac{1}{2}$ pound dry pasta to make 4 cups of cooked pasta. First heat 3 quarts of water to boiling in a large pot. Slowly add the pasta. Return to a full boil and cover the pot. Turn off the heat. Let the pasta sit for 8 to 12 minutes, or for the cooking time listed on the package instructions. Drain the pasta in a colander in the sink. Use immediately, or store in a plastic container in the refrigerator for later use.

Sweetie Treats and Freezer Pleasers

6

This chapter is full of super-delicious dessert recipes. Make them and eat them after school, after dinner, for breakfast, or whenever you want to mash and smash a treat that's sweet. As usual, you'll find easy-to-make recipes at the beginning and middle of the chapter and the more challenging recipes at the end. Be sure to try the Invent-a-Recipe for Freezie Sweets on page 110.

What's Inside:

Nanaberry Smash

Mash and smash bananas and berries for this tasty yogurt treat.

Makes 4 servings

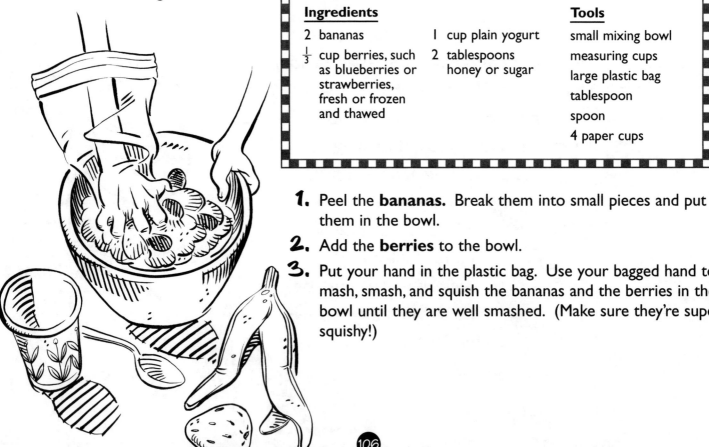

Ingredients

2 bananas

$\frac{1}{3}$ cup berries, such as blueberries or strawberries, fresh or frozen and thawed

1 cup plain yogurt

2 tablespoons honey or sugar

Tools

small mixing bowl

measuring cups

large plastic bag

tablespoon

spoon

4 paper cups

1. Peel the **bananas.** Break them into small pieces and put them in the bowl.

2. Add the **berries** to the bowl.

3. Put your hand in the plastic bag. Use your bagged hand to mash, smash, and squish the bananas and the berries in the bowl until they are well smashed. (Make sure they're super squishy!)

In banana-farmer talk, bananas are called fingers and bunches of bananas are called hands. So, go ahead—mash some fingers and have a Nanaberry Smash Bash!

4. Add the **yogurt** and **honey** to the smashed banana-berries. Stir well with the spoon.

5. Put 4 or 5 tablespoons of the yogurt and fruit mixture into each paper cup.

6. Serve your Nanaberry Smash right away, or freeze it for 2 to 3 hours.

Nickabuck Crunch Cups

Makes 2 servings

Make your own frozen yogurt treat—and say Nickabuck Crunch Cup five times fast.

Ingredients	Tools
5 graham cracker squares ($2\frac{1}{2}$ whole crackers)	small, sturdy, resealable plastic bag 2 paper cups
2 tablespoons cream cheese	small mixing bowl measuring cup
$\frac{1}{2}$ cup plain or vanilla yogurt	measuring spoons small spoon
3 tablespoons maple syrup	

1. Put the **graham crackers** into the plastic bag. Push the air out of the bag and seal it.

2. Pound and smash the bag with your hands and fingers. Do this until the crackers are well smashed. Pour the smashed crackers into the small bowl.

3. Add the **cream cheese** to the smashed graham crackers in the bowl. Smush well with your fingers until you've formed a doughlike mixture.

4. Put half the graham cracker–cream cheese dough in each paper cup. Use your fingers to press the mixture to cover the bottom and the sides of each cup.

5. Put the **yogurt** and the **maple syrup** in the small bowl. Stir well with the spoon.

6. Pour half of the yogurt mixture into each paper cup.

7. Freeze your Nickabuck Crunch Cups in the freezer for 2 to 3 hours.

Jamsicles

Makes 4 servings

Here's a sweet and simple frozen yogurt-sicle.

Ingredients	Tools	
$\frac{3}{4}$ cup plain or vanilla yogurt	measuring cup	small spoon
4 tablespoons of your favorite jam	measuring spoons	4 Popsicle molds
	small mixing bowl	

Invent-a-Recipe

Try making frosty cold Freezie Sweets. Just use your favorite combination of fruits, yogurts, jellies, juices, milk, crunchies, and anything else you'd like to freeze, in place of the ingredients in this recipe. Spoon your mixture into paper cups, baking cups, ice cube trays, Popsicle molds, or cupcake tins, and freeze in the freezer for 2 to 3 hours.

1. Put the **yogurt** and **jam** in the bowl. Stir well with the spoon.

2. Spoon an equal amount of the yogurt-jam mixture into each popsicle mold.

3. Freeze your Jamsicles in the freezer for 2 to 3 hours.

Nutsos

**Makes about 12 Nutsos
(4 to 6 servings)**

Peanuts are very popular today. Archaeologists have discovered that they were also popular in South America a long, long time ago. The archaeologists found jars shaped like peanuts in ancient mummy graves in Peru.

You'll go nuts for these nutty peanut butter balls.

Ingredients

$\frac{1}{2}$ cup peanuts

$\frac{1}{2}$ cup unsweetened peanut butter

3 tablespoons honey

4 tablespoons dried milk

crispy rice cereal (about 1 cup)

Tools

measuring cups

measuring spoons

large mixing bowl

large spoon

small bowl

plate

1. Put the **peanuts, peanut butter, honey,** and **dried milk** in the large mixing bowl. Stir well with the large spoon.

2. Pour the **crispy rice cereal** into the small bowl.

3. Pull off a piece of peanut mixture and roll it into a ball a little bigger than a giant gumball.

4. Roll the peanut ball in the cereal and put it on the plate.

5. Repeat steps 3 and 4 until you run out of the peanut mixture.

6. Chill your Nutsos in the refrigerator or eat them right away.

Triangle Blues

You won't sing the blues when you eat these jammy, creamy snacks.

Makes 1 or 2 servings

Ingredients	Tools	
1 pita bread	toaster oven	small bowl
$\frac{1}{4}$ cup blueberry jam	foil	small spoon
2 tablespoons cream cheese	cutting board	oven mitts
	table knife	timer
	measuring cup	spatula
	measuring spoons	plate

1. Remove the tray from the toaster oven. Cover it with foil and set it aside.

2. Preheat the toaster oven to broil.

BLUEBERRY JAM

To make your Triangle Blues in the microwave oven, follow steps 3 through 5, then put the stuffed triangles on a microwave-safe plate. Heat in the microwave for 30 seconds on high. Put on oven mitts to remove the plate from the microwave. Cool your snacks for 1 to 2 minutes before serving.

TIP

3. Put the **pita bread** on the cutting board. Use the table knife to cut the pita in half. Cut each half in half to make 4 triangles.

4. Put the **blueberry jam** and the **cream cheese** in the bowl. Mash together well with the spoon.

5. Stuff each pita triangle with about 1 tablespoon of the blueberry-cheese mixture.

6. Put the stuffed pita triangles on the foil-covered toaster oven tray.

7. Put on oven mitts and put the tray back in the toaster oven.

8. Heat the pita triangles for 2 to 3 minutes, or until lightly browned. Watch them carefully!

9. Wearing oven mitts, use a spatula to remove the pita triangles from the toaster oven, and put them on the plate. (Be sure to turn off the toaster oven.) Let cool for 1 to 2 minutes.

Mini Applesauce Pies

Cinnamon and graham crackers make these tiny pies taste great!

Makes 1 or 2 servings

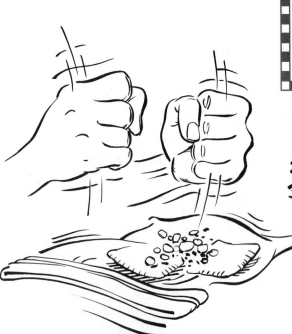

Ingredients

- 1 graham cracker (2 squares)
- $\frac{1}{4}$ cup applesauce
- 1 tablespoon raisins
- 3 shakes cinnamon
- 2 teaspoons brown sugar, packed
- 1 pita bread

Tools

- toaster oven
- foil
- small, sturdy resealable plastic bag
- small bowl
- measuring cups
- measuring spoons
- small spoon
- table knife
- cutting board
- oven mitts
- timer
- spatula
- plate

1. Remove the tray from the toaster oven. Cover it with foil and set it aside.

2. Preheat the toaster oven to medium broil.

3. Put the **graham cracker** into the plastic bag. Push the air out of the bag and seal it.

To make your Mini Applesauce Pies in the microwave oven, follow steps 3 through 7 to make the stuffed triangles. Put the stuffed triangles on a microwave-safe plate, and heat in the microwave for 30 seconds on high. Put on oven mitts to remove the plate from microwave. Let cool for 1 to 2 minutes before serving.

TIP

4. Pound and smash the bag with your fists until the graham cracker is well smashed. Put the smashed graham cracker into the small bowl.

5. Add the **applesauce, raisins, cinnamon,** and **brown sugar** to the bowl. Stir well with the spoon.

6. Put the **pita bread** on the cutting board. Use the table knife to cut the pita bread in half. Cut each half in half to make 4 triangles.

7. Stuff 1 heaping tablespoon of the applesauce mixture into each pita triangle.

8. Put the stuffed triangles on the foil-covered toaster oven tray.

9. Put on oven mitts and put the tray back in the toaster oven.

10. Heat the pita triangles for 2 to 3 minutes, or until lightly browned. Watch carefully!

11. Wearing oven mitts, use a spatula to remove your Mini Applesauce Pies from the toaster oven and put them on the plate. Let cool for 1 to 2 minutes.

Apple Bread Pudding Cups

Use a microwave oven to make these quick, delicious treats.

Makes 6 servings

Ingredients

1 egg

$\frac{1}{3}$ cup milk

$\frac{1}{3}$ cup applesauce

1 tablespoon brown sugar

1 tablespoon raisins

2 shakes cinnamon

2 slices bread

Tools

small mixing bowl

measuring spoons

spoon

6 paper baking cups

microwave-safe plate

oven mitts

timer

---

1. Crack the **egg** into the bowl.

2. Add the **milk, applesauce, brown sugar, raisins,** and **cinnamon** to the bowl. Stir well with the spoon.

3. Break the **bread** into small pieces. Put the bread pieces in the bowl and stir well.

4. Put about 2 tablespoons of the bread mixture into each baking cup.

5. Put the filled baking cups on the microwave-safe plate.

6. Put the plate in the microwave oven and heat for $1\frac{1}{2}$ minutes on high.

7. Put on oven mitts and remove the plate from the microwave oven. Let cool for 1 to 2 minutes before serving.

Banana Rice Pudding

This creamy rice pudding is wonderful served warm or cold.

Makes 4 servings

Ingredients	Tools	
I egg	medium mixing bowl	heavy-bottomed
2 cups cooked rice, brown or white	fork	2-quart pot
I cup milk	measuring cups	oven mitts
$\frac{1}{4}$ cup raisins	measuring spoons	timer
2 tablespoons brown sugar	wooden spoon	adult helper
2 shakes cinnamon		
I ripe banana		

1. Crack the **egg** into the bowl. Use the fork to mix well.

2. Add the **rice, milk, raisins, brown sugar,** and **cinnamon** to the bowl. Stir well with the wooden spoon.

3. Peel the **banana** and break it into small pieces. Add the banana pieces to the bowl and stir well.

4. Pour the banana-rice mixture into the pot.

5. Ask an adult to help you cook the rice mixture over medium high heat, stirring constantly with the wooden spoon. Cook the mixture until it thickens into a pudding, about 8 minutes.

6. Have the adult remove the pot from the heat. Let the pudding cool for 3 to 5 minutes.

119

Thumbprint Cookies

Make your mark in these crunchy jam-filled cookies.

Makes about 20 cookies

Ingredients

2 teaspoons margarine

1 cup quick oats (not instant)

1 cup flour, white or whole wheat

$\frac{1}{3}$ cup wheat germ

$\frac{3}{4}$ cup brown sugar, packed

$\frac{1}{2}$ teaspoon cinnamon

1 teaspoon baking powder

$\frac{1}{2}$ teaspoon baking soda

$\frac{3}{4}$ cup chopped walnuts

1 egg

$\frac{1}{2}$ cup vegetable oil

1 tablespoon water

$\frac{1}{4}$ cup of your favorite fruit jam

Tools

small piece of waxed paper

measuring spoons

2 cookie sheets

measuring cups

large mixing bowl

small, sturdy resealable plastic bag

rolling pin

small bowl

fork

large spoon

timer

oven mitts

adult helper

1. Preheat the oven to 375°F.

2. Use the waxed paper and **margarine** to grease both cookie sheets. Set them aside.

People made the first flour 75,000 years ago by roasting edible seeds from wild plants and then mashing and smashing the seeds with rocks.

3. Put the **quick oats, flour, wheat germ, brown sugar, cinnamon, baking powder,** and **baking soda** into the mixing bowl. Mix well with your hands. Use your fingers to smash all of the brown sugar lumps.

4. Put the **walnuts** into the plastic bag. Push the air out of the bag and seal it.

5. Use the rolling pin to bash and smash the nuts until they are very well smashed.

6. Pour the smashed nuts into the flour-oat mixture. Use your hands to mix well.

7. Crack the **egg** into the small bowl. Mix well with the fork.

8. Pour the egg into the flour-oat mixture.

9. Add the **oil** and **water** to the bowl. Stir well with the large spoon.

10. Use your hands to mix together all the ingredients in the bowl to form a moist, crumbly cookie dough.

11. Take a little bit of the dough, about the size of a giant gumball, and roll it into a ball. Put it on the cookie sheet.

12. Repeat step 11 until you've used up all of the cookie dough. Put 8 to 12 balls on each cookie sheet, leaving 1 to

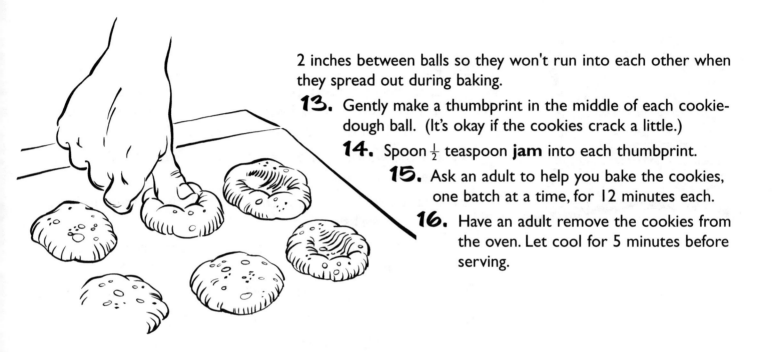

2 inches between balls so they won't run into each other when they spread out during baking.

13. Gently make a thumbprint in the middle of each cookie-dough ball. (It's okay if the cookies crack a little.)

14. Spoon $\frac{1}{2}$ teaspoon **jam** into each thumbprint.

15. Ask an adult to help you bake the cookies, one batch at a time, for 12 minutes each.

16. Have an adult remove the cookies from the oven. Let cool for 5 minutes before serving.

Index